BREAKING NEW GROUND

AMERICAN WOMEN
1800-1848

THE YOUNG OXFORD HISTORY OF WOMEN IN THE UNITED STATES

Nancy F. Cott, *General Editor*

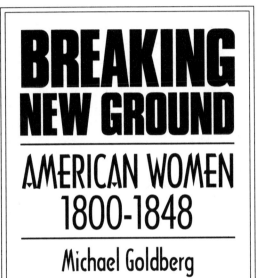

BREAKING NEW GROUND

AMERICAN WOMEN
1800-1848

Michael Goldberg

OXFORD UNIVERSITY PRESS

New York • Oxford

To Elizabeth
Love, Michael

Oxford University Press

Oxford   New York   Toronto
Delhi   Bombay   Calcutta   Madras   Karachi
Kuala Lumpur   Singapore   Hong Kong   Tokyo
Nairobi   Dar es Salaam   Cape Town
Melbourne   Auckland   Madrid
and associated companies in
Berlin   Ibadan
Copyright © 1994 by Michael Goldberg
Introduction copyright © 1994 by Oxford University Press, Inc.
Published by Oxford University Press, Inc., 200 Madison Avenue, New York, New York 10016
Oxford is a registered trademark of Oxford University Press, Inc.

Library of Congress Cataloging-in-Publication Data

Goldberg, Michael
Breaking new ground: American women 1800-1848 / Michael Goldberg.
p. cm. — (Young Oxford history of women in the United States; v. 4)
Includes bibliographical references and index.
ISBN 0-19-508202-8
ISBN 0-19-508830-1 (series)
1. Women—United States—History—19th century—Juvenile literature. 2. Women—United States—Social conditions—
Juvenile literature. 3. United States—Social conditions—Juvenile literature. [1. Women—History—19th century.
2. Women—Social conditions. 3. United States—Social conditions—To 1865.]
I. Title. II. Series
HQ1418.G65 1994
305.4'0973'09034—dc20   93-33739
                                                                              CIP
                                                                              AC

1 3 5 7 9 8 6 4 2

Printed in the United States of America
on acid-free paper

Design: Leonard Levitsky
Picture Research: Pat Burns, Laura Kreiss

On the cover: Corn Planting by Olof Krans, 1846.
Frontispiece: Mill workers from Lowell, Massachusetts.

CONTENTS

INTRODUCTION

I n 1800, social and political relationships in the United States were marked by deference. That meant that the "better sort"— those who had the advantages of birth, wealth, and educa- tion—were accustomed to leading the society, and the less well-off accepted and deferred to this leadership. By 1840, such ex- pectations of deference had notably lessened, especially in political life. Most states had stopped requiring that men be property holders in order to be qualified to vote, and as a result, the great majority of adult white men were eligible. Besides, the rise of political parties meant that politics became a great national passion, with a very high proportion of those eligible actually participating. Candidates for office now stressed their humble ("log cabin") origins in order to gain popular appeal.

This substantial democratization of the vote bypassed women (and all slaves) entirely. Yet women both participated in and were affected by the same ferment that produced the political "era of the common man." There were distinctive gender dimensions to the political changes of the era. As politics became less the domain of the "better sort" and more the domain of ordinary men, it became more obviously a *masculine* domain. Women's domain, in contrast, was not to be politics, but the home. In the 1820s and 1830s an outpouring of publications from American presses, written by min-

The Crowning of Flora, *painted by Jacob Marling in 1816, depicts a ceremony at a female seminary. By mid-century, seminaries and colleges were opening throughout the country to offer women a rigorous education similar to that provided to men.*

isters, publicists, moralists, and educators (both male and female), clarified a domestic ideal of womanhood. This model, widely accepted and diffused, promised that the virtuous wife and mother, by securing harmony in the home, by providing for her husband's comfort and her children's morality and good character, could assure social order in the tumultuous American scene. At the same time, some women found the domestic ideal inaccurate, inadequate, or constricting—for instance, industrial workers, hardscrabble pioneers, slaves, religious exhorters, and reformers who sought the end of slavery or the radical expansion of women's rights. As this book shows, some of these women seized the democratic promise of the age for themselves, contesting the harmonious domestic ideal of womanhood.

This book is part of a series that covers the history of women in the United States from the 17th through 20th century. Traditional historical writing has dealt almost entirely with men's lives because men have, until very recently, been the heads of state, the political officials, judges, ministers, and business leaders who have wielded the most visible and recorded power. But for several recent decades, new interest has arisen in social and cultural history, where common people are the actors who create trends and mark change as well as continuity. An outpouring of research and writing on women's history has been part of this trend to look at individuals and groups

This weaving room was part of a small New England textile mill. Most women workers, however, worked in larger mills, such as those in Lowell, Massachusetts, which typically employed about 800 people.

who have not held the reins of rule in their own hands but nonetheless participated in making history. The motive to address and correct sexual inequality in society has also vitally influenced women's history, on the thinking that knowledge of the past is essential to creating justice for the future.

The histories in this series look at many aspects of women's lives. The books ask new questions about the course of American history. How did the type and size of families change, and what difference did that make in people's lives? What expectations for women differed from those for men, and how did such expectations change over the centuries? What roles did women play in the economy? What form did women's political participation take when they could not vote? And how did politics change when women did gain full citizenship? How did women work with other women who were like or unlike them, as well as with men, for social and political goals? What sex-specific constraints or opportunities did they face? The series aims to understand the diverse women who have peopled American history by investigating their work and leisure, family patterns, political activities, forms of organization, and outstanding accomplishments. Standard events of American history, from the settling of the continent to the American revolution, the Civil War, industrialization, American entry onto the world stage, and world wars, are all here, too, but seen from the point of view of women's experiences. Together, the answers to new questions and the treatment of old ones from women's points of view make up a compelling narrative of four centuries of history in the United States.

—Nancy F. Cott

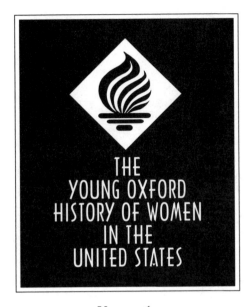

THE YOUNG OXFORD HISTORY OF WOMEN IN THE UNITED STATES

CHAPTER 1

REASONS OF THE HEART: MARRIAGE AND COURTSHIP

Elizabeth Endicott's courtship with Timothy Pickering was a long, difficult business. At least that is how Pickering saw it. Like Timothy, Elizabeth was born and raised in the small town of Hadley, Massachusetts. Her grandparents had been prosperous farmers. Her father now owned a dry goods store, while her mother managed the household. At the time Timothy began to court her she had just turned 22 and finished several terms at a female seminary. For three years, Pickering, the son of a Congregationalist minister, had been seeking Elizabeth's hand in marriage. During that time, the couple had sent a constant stream of letters back and forth. Again and again, Timothy professed his love for "my most precious evening star, my most beloved, my most treasured Elizabeth."

Elizabeth responded to these flowery words cautiously, trying to gauge what a future with Timothy would be like. Even though she had known him since childhood, she had only recently considered him as a mate for life. She backed out of the relationship several times, once insisting that she was not worthy of his love. To a friend she bemoaned her inability to accept the love that Timothy seemed to offer so unreservedly. Finally, after Timothy threatened to break off the relationship unless she answered yes or no, she consented, and they were soon married.

During the 19th century, women were encouraged to marry for love and companionship.

Nettie Harris's courtship was less complicated. Raised on a farm in upper New York State, Nettie saw how her parents had to work harder every year to compete with the newer, more productive farms in the West. Since the greatest opportunities seemed to be in the West, she decided to head that way herself. Eighteen years old, Nettie had little formal schooling; she had spent most of her youth working on her parents' farm, learning the skills necessary for a farm woman.

She had been lured west by an advertisement in a local newspaper that proclaimed, "Every respectable young woman who goes to the West is almost sure of an advantageous marriage, while, from the superabundance of her own sex in the east, her chances for success are not greater than those for a disappointment." Nettie no doubt thought herself respectable. As to motivation, she had little money (and thus nothing to lose) and the adventurousness that comes with youth.

After leaving her New York home, she found herself with some 40 other women traveling on a flatboat to Iowa. Upon arriving at the dock of her destination, this group was met in the manner described by a magazine of the time:

> The gentlemen on shore make proposals to the ladies through trumpets:
>
> "Miss with the blue ribbon in your bonnet, will you take me?"
> "Hallo that girl with a cinnamon-colored shawl! If agreeable we will join!"
>
> The ladies in the meantime are married at the hotel, the parties arranging themselves as the squire sings out, "Sort yourselves, sort yourselves!"

No sooner had Nettie arrived by flatboat in frontier Iowa than she found herself a match.

Louisa Briggs's courtship took less time than Elizabeth Endicott's, but it was no less well supervised. Born into slavery in the South, Louisa grew up on a medium-sized plantation in Virginia, where she was sent to work in the fields by the age of 12. Her father and several brothers had been sold away by her master to a distant plantation, but the rest of her extended family—mothers, sisters and other brothers, grandparents, aunts and uncles—provided her with support growing up. When she was 16, her master began to offer hints that he expected Louisa to find a mate, and more important, to begin bearing children.

A somewhat idealized view of slave courtship by artist Eastman Johnson. Slaves had little time or opportunity for courtship, but older relatives and friends made sure young couples were chaperoned.

Her young suitor, Thomas Cole, lived on a nearby plantation, where he worked as a driver, a supervisory position that carried with it a great deal of prestige. Thomas went through intense negotiations with his master to get permission to leave the plantation every Sunday to go courting. His master had hoped that Thomas would find a wife on his own plantation, but gave in when it was clear that Thomas, who was a valued worker, would be greatly demoralized if he was not able to pursue the woman who had won his heart.

Louisa's mother, Maria, was impressed with Thomas's passion and position, but still insisted that the couple take things slowly. Maria chaperoned the young couple every time they "visited." Louisa herself was quite taken with her admirer, but wondered what life would be like without a husband nearby except on Sundays. Unless Louisa's master bought Thomas—and he would command a high price—they would have only their weekly visits together. But Maria counseled her daughter that there were some advantages to this arrangement. "A man can be a fine thing to have handy, but then he can be more than his share of trouble. You see him one day a week, you'll appreciate him the more."

After two months of courtship, Thomas asked Louisa to marry him, and she agreed. Louisa then quickly received her master's permission about her choice of a mate. He was only too happy to own Thomas's offspring, as the young driver had proven himself to be a fine worker and physical specimen.

Very different rituals, these, with very different meanings.

Even though Elizabeth, Nettie, and Louisa are composite characters, not actual individuals who lived in the early 19th century, their lives accurately represent the trials and triumphs of real women of that time. Their hopes and concerns about courtship and marriage were typical of the women who lived in America at the time. And the changes taking place in such personal relationships reflected changes in society at large.

Before the Industrial Revolution, which began in the 1790s in New England and would transform an overwhelmingly agricultural society into an industrial one, most people had made their living off the land as farmers or livestock producers. However, as the Industrial Revolution got under way, and American entrepreneurs harnessed the energy of New England's many rivers to provide water power for textile mills, more and more people worked in factories and offices of the growing towns and cities of the Northeast.

Industrialization had helped create an urban middle class whose members had more money to spend than their grandparents. Middle-class families used their greater earnings to purchase ready-made goods—everything from soap to shoes—that were once produced by women in these families. Further, more urban men worked in shops and offices than on the land. Finally, middle-class people no longer needed large families to help them work the farm. Indeed, a large family could now be seen as an economic burden.

Before the American Revolution, New Englanders viewed the family as a strict hierarchy, an arrangement in which power flowed from top to bottom: The father was ruler of all, the mother was underneath him, and the (theoretically) obedient children were at the bottom. After 1800, however, that ideal changed. Book and magazine writers began picturing families in which men controlled the public realm of politics and business, but women took responsibility for the private sphere of the home. A marriage was viewed more as a partnership; true, the woman was still the junior partner, but the older model of the man as absolute ruler was no longer fashionable among middle-class Northeasterners. Yet despite women's

TWO SPHERES OF LIFE.

In this satirical print, a woman's life is divided into doing housework and learning social skills, such as how to play a musical instrument. She does not enter the public sphere of life dominated by men.

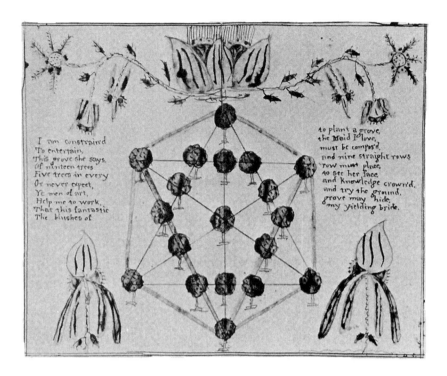

This watercolor from the early 1800s was sent by a suitor to a young woman to express his love and desire. Love letters were part of the elaborate courtship rituals of white, middle-class couples.

newly glorified power within the home, they still could not vote, nor own property in their name once married, nor file a lawsuit, nor execute a will.

The changing view of marriage helps us understand Elizabeth Endicott's reluctance to marry. As marriage was seen as more of a partnership, courtship became a time to prove the existence of extraordinary compatibility and radiant love. As a woman in Catherine Sedgewick's popular novel *Clarence* (1830) put it, "Ever since I first thought of it at all, I have always said I would never marry any man that I was not willing to die for." Since perfect men did not pass through one's life every day, those women who aimed high were in for a certain amount of intellectual and emotional anguish before they made their final choice.

A couple's courtship unfolded like an elaborate chess game. It was up to the women to establish the bounds of decency and mutual self-respect while encouraging the love professed by the man. Society had quite clearly drawn the line at sexual intercourse; anything up to that point, however, was for the couple to decide.

The opportunities were many. Indeed, one favorite activity of courting couples—known as "bundling"—allowed them to sleep in the same bed unchaperoned. One suitor, Elias Nason, wrote of "all the walks and kisses and larks and sings and thoughts and meetings and partings and clingings" that he and his sweetheart had shared. His fiancée, responding to one of his love letters, replied, "O! I really do want to kiss you. . . . How I should like to be in that old parlor with you . . . I hope there will be a carpet on the floor for it seems you intend to act worse than you ever did before your letter . . . but I shall humbly submit to my fate and willingly too, to speak candidly."

A sailor on a New England whaling ship made this whalebone carving of a marriage proposal. Although most women desired marriage, many were uneasy about giving up control of their lives to a husband.

At some point during this struggle over sex, a man was expected to propose to his beloved. One woman noted that it was "true we have the liberty of refusing those we don't like, but not of selecting those we do." If a woman were forthright in her interest for a man, she would be instantly labeled an immoral adventuress. This too would bring her respectability rating down several notches, thus lessening her marriage prospects.

Because the man felt he was putting so much on the line by proposing, a "proper" woman was expected to return a well-reasoned reply within a short period of time. A woman knew, however, that her response was perhaps her last chance to have control over her life. Once she said "yes," the legal cards would be stacked against her, regardless of the declarations of love by her suitor. Because the expectations of middle-class marriage had been raised so high, women found reports of marital disasters very disconcerting. One married woman wrote to a single friend that marriage was "a sad, sour, sober beverage" that brought "some joys, but many crosses."

Numerous women suffered "marriage trauma," spending days or weeks depressed and emotionally paralyzed at the thought of their impending commitment. Women well understood their relative powerlessness once they said "yes." Hannah Hunnington, a young New England woman, wrote to her fiancé, "Every joy in anticipation depends on you, and from you must I derive every pleasure." Mary Windsor, a New Hampshire woman, bemoaned, "O, it is solemn, it is awful, thus to bind one's self for life."

The wedding was planned quickly once a couple made the decision to marry. The wedding celebration, or lack of it, showed that in the Northeast the ceremony was in part about the triumph of restraint over pleasure. Weddings were often performed during the

A farm wedding involved the expectation that both husband and wife would contribute crucial labor to the running of the farm.

week so they would not interfere with the minister's Sabbath duties. The date was announced a week or two before the ceremony, and the gathering was limited to friends and family from the area. Even when middle-class weddings became more elaborate after the 1830s, the atmosphere of restraint still prevailed.

Once married, the suitors often cooled the fiery protestations of love found in their letters. Although many couples developed strong, deep bonds of affection, the idea of separate spheres—that women should stay at home, and men go out in the world—kept them apart for many hours of their lives. Advice books and religious sermons emphasized that wives were to make the home a haven of restfulness for their husbands.

This separation of duties provided women with other companionship, however. The split between home and work strengthened friendships between women as they came to understand what they shared with each other and how their lives differed from men's. Unlike a wife's relationship with her husband, a friendship with another woman was based on equality. Although women developed networks of friends and relatives, intense relationships between two women were not uncommon.

A successful marriage for a woman like Hannah Hunnington was one in which the husband was prudent with his money and gracious toward his wife. A disastrous marriage was one in which

An 1850s quilting party in western Virginia gives farm wives and daughters a chance to mingle with neighbors. These gatherings allowed women to escape temporarily the isolation of farm life.

the man drank, managed his money poorly, and physically and verbally abused his wife and children. Only in the most extreme cases—when a man was guilty of desertion, violence against his wife or children, flagrant adultery, or well-documented alcoholism—could a woman hope to divorce her husband. Although divorces were growing faster among the urban northern middle class than any other group, such separations were still rare. Within the United States, only one in a thousand marriages ended in divorce before the Civil War.

If a woman successfully sued for divorce, she would soon be wondering what price she had paid for her freedom. Alimony, or money paid regularly by a husband to his former wife, was rarely awarded, although judges occasionally ordered one-time cash settlements to women who had been abused by their husbands. If a woman had brought property into the marriage, she was not likely to take it back out. Once she and her husband said their "I do's," her husband legally controlled all she owned. Her chances for finding work were few, especially if she was approaching or beyond middle age.

Before 1800, a divorced woman could not even have gained custody of her children, since most judges believed that fathers were the "natural custodians" of their offspring. The new ideal of domesticity, of women's "natural" place as guardian of the home, reversed this trend, so that now judges began to cite women's "unique capacity" for nurturing their children. Unfortunately, the law did not back

In this cartoon, a woman snubs her nose at her former husband after their divorce. In reality, however, divorce was a last resort for women, especially if children were involved, because the laws did not require the husband to pay for child support.

this concept up with provisions for child support. Even though divorce offered huge disadvantages for a woman, many a battered or scorned middle-class wife was glad that the option existed and was becoming more accepted.

Even the best of northeastern marriages demanded that a woman deny many of her own ambitions in order to serve her husband and children. Yet for women the promise of idealized love remained, as did the notion of women as morally superior to men. These ideas gave northeastern middle-class women a greater sense of possibilities for their role in the community and nation. Women came to understand that they, as a group distinctive from men, had something to offer society that men did not. These women realized that they could be the nurturers, the moral educators, of their country. As America expanded, so too did these women's vision of their place in the home, and the home's place in the world.

Conditions on the prairies of the northern frontier—covering the states of Ohio, Indiana, Illinois, Missouri, and Iowa—were quite unlike those in the small-town and urban Northeast. The prairie frontier was overwhelmingly agricultural, but because farming was such hard work, only a few women—most of them widows—worked the land without a husband.

Although frontier women, unlike their northeastern sisters, rarely suffered from marriage trauma, this does not mean they were not careful in choosing a spouse. Frontier women hoped to find a man who was hardworking, thrifty, and eventempered. Lucinda Casteen, a frontierswoman writing to her sister in Kentucky, advised her, "it will be in your interest to come or go where you can have a home of your own, but never give your hand or heart to a lazy man."

Not many frontiersmen attempted to run their farms without a wife. A man might clear the land and plant the crops for a few years alone, but there were few who acknowledged the charms of "baching." Bachelor farmers became married farmers in short order as they realized that it was extremely difficult to make a farm pay without the help of women. Bachelors also found that life on the prairie could get terribly lonely, with no companionship and neighbors many miles away.

The nature of farming meant that women and men worked the same land, that women helped produce food and earn cash. Women thus saw the farm as a mutual effort. Frontier women were also less

The children are the wife's primary concern in this 1801 portrait of Nathan Hawley and his family. As Northeastern women assumed responsibility for the home, they took control of their children's development and moral education.

concerned than their eastern contemporaries with raising perfect families. On the frontier, children were valued as workers and companions. These conditions made for a more pragmatic approach to child rearing.

Children were an important part of the work force on a prairie farm. While the size of northeastern middle-class families was shrinking dramatically during this period, frontier families were holding steady, averaging around seven children each. Compared to northeastern women, frontier women married earlier, had children earlier, and continued to give birth for more years—often past the age of 45. But whereas northeastern women might have seen family size as a choice to be negotiated with their husbands, frontier women had no such options. They considered a large family just another part of life on the prairie.

Giving birth to numerous children increased a woman's chance of dying in childbirth; it also made for some very busy years when the children were still young. As Frances Trollope, an Englishwoman who lived for several years in the frontier town of Cincinnati, noted, "You continually see women with infants on their knee, that you feel sure are their grand-children, till some convincing proof of the contrary is displayed. Even the young girls, though often with lovely features, look pale, thin and haggard."

Though the lives of northern and frontier women differed from

Mountaineers celebrate a young couple's wedding announcement. Although the bride looks frail and shy, frontier life required that women develop much physical strength and stamina.

A MOUNTAIN TRIP

each other in some ways, both stood in stark contrast to the lives of southern slave women. For instance, Louisa Briggs, living as a slave in the South, was physically vulnerable to a culture in which violence was an everyday and often random occurrence. Slaves could be whipped or even tortured by their masters for misdeeds real or imagined.

Slave women were also vulnerable to sexual advances and attacks by their masters, overseers, or masters' sons. Although those slaveholders professing Christian values officially condemned such "race mixing," they also knew that sexual contact between black women and white men was commonplace. One needed only to look at the large number of mulatto children on any plantation to prove it. In order to shift the blame away from slaveholders, some whites insisted that black women, being "naturally" sexually aggressive, were often as not the seducers. Slaveholders must be wary of such temptations, urged one white preacher, and not fall prey to such enticements.

Slaveholder fantasies aside, most sexual relations between white men and black women were the result of some form of white coercion. Many masters believed that sexual relations with their slaves was simply a right of ownership.

Marriage relations between enslaved African Americans in the South changed little during the early 19th century. Legally, a master

The brutality of the slave system attempted to dehumanize blacks and made every aspect of their lives subject to a master's control. Even getting married or establishing a family was difficult if the master did not consent.

owned a slave and could compel that person to do whatever he wished. However, most slaveholders wanted their slaves to pair off and often sanctioned slave unions with their blessing, but marriages between slaves were not recognized legally. Nonetheless, most slave owners had at least one eye on their finances in supporting a slave's choice in marriage. A typical plantation manual advised slaveholders that a slave marriage based on love would add "to the comfort, happiness and health of those entering upon it, besides ensuring greater increase." Such marriages produced both stability and more slaves, two requirements of a successful plantation operation.

How, amidst this brutal system, could African-American women and men nurture love and commitment? Love may not triumph over everything, but the romantic love that many black women and men felt for each other did indeed endure slavery. What brought most slave couples together was physical and emotional attraction. Lucy Ann Dunn, a slave from North Carolina, remembered the thrill of her courtship: "It was in the little Baptist church where I first seen big black Jim Dunn and I fell in love with him then I reckon. He said that he loved me then too, but it was three Saturdays before he asked to see me home." Both Jim and Lucy were careful to adhere to the mores of their culture. Lucy recalled:

> We walked that mile home in front of my Mammy, and I was so happy that I ain't thought it half a mile home. We ate corn bread and turnips for dinner, and it was night before he went home. Mammy wouldn't let me walk with him to the gate, I knowed, so I just sat there on the porch and says goodnight. He come every Sunday for a year and finally he proposed. I told Mammy that I thought that I ought to be allowed to walk to the gate with Jim and she said all right, if she was settin' there on the porch lookin'.

Although many black couples exhibited as much restraint as middle-class couples up North, it was not uncommon for children to be born out of wedlock because slave culture did not make outcasts of unwed mothers. Instead, the slave community expected the new father and mother to wed, whereupon the newborn was immediately accepted into the community. Black couples made an extra effort to respect personal boundaries in an effort to replace some measure of the self-respect their owners tried to strip from them. Indeed, a number of white observers noted that while slave couples often adhered to Christian notions of sexual restraint, their aggressive masters frequently did not.

Slaves viewed marriage as a means to build community stability. Despite the inherent tragedy of the situation—that two people were to bring their offspring into an unfree world—slaves rose above their oppression and the size of their community increased.

Weddings were both solemn and joyous occasions. At a minimum, a conscientious master would contribute some whiskey, and

This marriage license was issued to a free black couple in Virginia in 1807. Slave marriages, by contrast, were not considered legal unions.

perhaps a hog or two. If the slave were a favorite of the master or mistress—particularly if the bride was a personal servant of the mistress—the slaveholder would sponsor the wedding. These were more elaborate affairs, with goodly quantities of food or drink, dancing and singing.

A slave wedding combined African with Anglo-Christian traditions. A common ritual was the broomstick ceremony, in which couples finalized the deal by leaping over a broomstick together. In one version, the bride and groom took their separate turns to determine who would be "the boss of the marriage." Tempie Herndon was so inspired to avoid an unequal marriage that she recalled that she "sailed right over that broomstick same as a cricket."

Although slaves were not legally bound together, they usually stayed together. A marriage that had been arranged by the master was usually doomed, but those based on mutual love prospered. The slave community saw adultery by either the woman or the man as a serious transgression. Because slave men owned so little, and generally received their food, clothing, and shelter from their masters, slave women were less economically bound to their husbands than white women were. Slave marriages thus proceeded on a more equal basis than most white marriages.

All too often, masters separated slave families by selling different members off to faraway plantations. Many slaveholders professed a belief in the sanctity of the marriage covenant. Other slaveholders, however, cared little for the niceties of family ties, and were willing to sell whichever slave might bring a profit. Even those adhering to moral beliefs about marriage might break up a family to pay off debts. And when a master died, there were no guarantees that a slave family's rights would be acknowledged.

Despite these threats to the slave family—in fact because of them—slave women and men fought to create and maintain a stable family. If a family member was sold away to a distant plantation, she or he would instantly be adopted by a network of "aunts," "uncles," and "cousins." And when the Civil War ended, newly freed slaves traveled across the South in search of the husbands and wives who had been torn from them.

For many plantation mistresses, staging an elaborate slave wedding was a chance to relive their own moment of glory. Their wedding was their crowning moment; it was also the benchmark of their decline. Southern plantation women married earlier than northern women, usually around the age of 20. By their mid-20s, when middle-class Northerners were marrying, single plantation women were being labeled "old maids." The southern "belle" was spared nothing by her doting parents—she could purchase the latest fash-

Slaveholders often considered economics to be more important than the ties of slave families. Here, a mother and child are separated as the master prepares to sell the mother at auction.

Godey's Lady's Book for August 1843 printed this fashion plate as an example of what well-dressed women should wear. These dresses were made of silk and muslin, trimmed with lace, artificial flowers, and other frills.

ions, then quickly discard them for a new ensemble. She lived in a sheltered world, punctuated by frequent balls and daily rounds of social calls to other fashionable women in the neighborhood.

Plantation parents kept a much more watchful eye on their charges than their counterparts to the North. One observer noted that in contrast to Northerners, "in the South it is deemed indecorous for them to be left alone, and the mother or some member of the family is always in the room; and if none of these, a female slave is seated on the rug at the door."

If sex was out, flirting was expected, and many belles raised it to an art form. One belle, Cary Bryon, declared "she meant to have as many lovers as she could bring to her feet to be a reputed belle." For Cary, "lovers" were of the verbal variety only, supplemented by an occasional well-chaperoned peck on the cheek. One Southerner wrote to another about a friend whose "wife never took his arm till she took it to be led to the church on her wedding day, and that he never had an opportunity of kissing her but twice" before the ceremony.

Unlike her northern cousins, belles did not reject marriage proposals because of feelings of inadequacy as future mothers, but simply as a matter of course. If, in her rejection, the belle held out any hope at all of relenting, the young man took this first refusal as merely the opening salvo in a long campaign.

If a woman's "honor" was violated, an overly aggressive suitor could expect to get a call from an enraged brother or father. If the young man was fortunate, the avenger would not shoot at once, but would merely insist upon a duel at ten paces. Within the plantation class, then, a belle could flirt at will without doing damage to her character. It was for the male suitor to maintain the honor of southern white women, or else suffer the consequences. This offered southern plantation women some protection against marauding men, but it also placed them, much more than their northern counterparts, in the role of helpless victim.

For both the belle and the suitor, financial considerations played an important role in the final selection of a marriage partner. It was not uncommon for a man to designate a monetary value on the object of his affection. One fellow, newly married and brimming with pride for his bride, noted that, besides her many "excellent qualities, she is worth $2,500. She has a good piece of land about 10 or 12 miles from Nashville." Another man, calculating his attraction to a prospective bride, wrote, "If she were not guilty of the unpardonable crime in Mississippi, to wit, poverty—would be a great belle. She is pretty and smart." Belles had as keen an eye for the financial bottom line as their male counterparts—many a poorly matched couple was the result of a young woman choosing financial prospects over character and temperament.

Eventually, the belle would settle on a favorite and the wedding date would be announced. Weddings were important moments in a society where social events played a central role in reaffirming a way of life. These were usually lavish affairs, with extensive guest lists and menus. Relatives from afar were expected to reunite with the family during these festivities. The big house was abuzz with preparations for a week before the celebration, and weddings between members of particularly important families were the source of neighborhood gossip for quite a while afterward.

Marriage relations among the southern planter class were in many ways an exaggerated version of those among the northeastern middle class. While virginity before marriage was expected for northeastern women, southern planter society placed an absolute premium on the bride's "purity." Northeastern women were placed on a platform and praised for their selflessness and moral rectitude. Plantation women were put upon a gilded pedestal, and southern writers extolled the refinement, piety, and grace by which these women surpassed all others. The result was a tightly constrained life that offered southern women few opportunities to move beyond the boundaries their society had established for them.

This vision of the plantation woman on a pedestal was created by the southern planter aristocracy to offset the violence and inhumanity of slavery. Plantation women thus experienced striking contradictions in their lives and their marriages. They often had to overlook their husbands' extramarital affairs, including sexual relations—forced or otherwise—with slave women; and they had to be the keepers of Christian piety while wielding the lash against unwilling servants. Their marriages prospered or faltered according to the degree to which they were able to rationalize these contradictions throughout their lives.

Despite the tensions inherent in the slavery system, many slaveholding couples managed to develop loving relationships. The strongest marriages were those in which the husband remained true to the Christian principles so many professed to support. In these marriages, the wife was a true partner in the plantation enterprise. The planter stuck by the vows of monogamy he made at his wedding, and kept at arm's length from the prevailing male culture of violence. For these men, time spent away from home was not an opportunity to play the rogue, but rather a cause for homesickness. "If I could grasp you to my bosom at this moment," wrote one forlorn traveler to his wife, "how happy should I be."

Mr. and Mrs. James Beaty of Vicksburg, Mississippi. Because Southern society demanded that women lead model lives of refinement and piety, many wives felt constrained in their role on the plantation.

The textile mills of New England offered relatively high wages and a sense of independence to young working women in the 19th century.

CHAPTER 2

WORKING IN THE HOME, WORKING IN THE FIELDS, WORKING FOR WAGES

With all the changes in women's lives from 1800 to the present, at least one thing has remained constant—housework is equated with women's work. Women still do most of the cooking, cleaning, and child-raising that goes on in private homes across the country. Now, however, many women also have the opportunity to work as doctors, social workers, secretaries, or even construction workers. In the early 19th century, women who worked outside the home had far fewer choices than women today, and they earned far less money. And in almost every case, the wage-paying work they did— teaching, textile manufacturing, domestic service—was connected to women's traditional work in the home.

Consider the very different wash days of Elizabeth Endicott and Nettie Harris, of New England and Illinois, respectively.

Suppose that Elizabeth Endicott, having married Thomas Pickering, proceeded to have three children. Thomas's dry goods store prospered, and he was able to buy Elizabeth the latest box stove, a relatively recent invention in 1830. His income also allowed him to buy a goodly supply of coal every month in order to heat the stove, and thus the water for washing. The water itself came from the pump in the front yard, which was drawn from their well.

If Elizabeth was lucky enough to have employed a "hired girl" to help her, she would have assigned her the task of drawing and carrying the water. This young woman—we'll call her Nell—then lit and maintained the fire for the stove, and heated the water in a large, heavy iron pot. Once the hot water had been poured into the manual washing machine, Elizabeth herself took control of the process, not trusting her servant to take proper care with the family's clothes. After washing that week's laundry, Nell, Elizabeth, and Elizabeth's oldest daughters attached the laundry to the clothesline outside with wooden clothespins, another recent invention. Once the sun had done its work, Elizabeth gathered the clothing and neatly folded each article.

If the wash day for a middle-class New Englander appears time-consuming to us today, imagine the enormity of Nettie Harris's task on the Illinois frontier. Nettie would probably be doing laundry not only for a larger family—upwards of eight children—but perhaps for a few seasonal workers as well. She would have been helped by her older children, but most likely she would not have had a paid servant; not only would cash be in short supply, but so would the available labor. Few women were willing to work as domestics on the frontier when marriage appeared to be a better option.

Nettie's husband split the wood for fuel from logs that he had felled earlier in the year. Nettie then dragged water in buckets from a nearby stream. She boiled her water over a fireplace, not a stove. Then she scrubbed each article of clothing against a washboard, using soap she and her daughters had made, before rinsing it in a separate tub.

This washing and wringing machine was advertised to housewives as a way to save the wear on clothes. Sewing and washing clothes consumed a large amount of every wife's time, even if she had help from servants.

Frontier women like Nettie also spent much of their time producing clothing. Few frontier women were without a spinning wheel and loom; these were the essential tools of the trade. Many an evening was spent bent over these machines, working steadily while teaching daughters the techniques that had been passed down from their grandmothers.

Homespun, as the fabric was called, was an important source of cash or barter. Since most of the money from raising crops and livestock went to pay off mortgages on the land, taxes, and farm equipment, homespun was used either to purchase manufactured goods from the East or to expand the farm operations. Charlotte Jacobs remembered that in order to acquire pigs for the farm, she "bought twelve shoats and paid for them with linsey and jeans of my own make." Other frontier women traded their excess homespun for clocks, pianos, and better butter churns, as well as additional land and implements. In this way a farm community worked itself out of the frontier stage of its development.

Besides the edible products of the garden, a farm woman managed the family poultry flock that provided meat and eggs, as well as down for quilts and pillows. She also fed and milked the cows, and then churned the cream into butter. When a steer was butchered, she used the fat to make soap and candles. She butchered hogs, then smoked and salted the meat. After harvest, she pickled, dried, and canned much of her garden produce for winter consumption.

Farm women living on the frontier rarely had time for leisure—the occasional church meeting or Fourth of July celebration were her only days off. Both she and her husband toiled from sunup to sundown to make their farm a paying proposition. But as her husband rested in the evening from his labor in the fields, a woman would be busy cleaning up after supper, spinning yarn, mending clothing, or entertaining the children. One observer, the French writer Alexis de Tocqueville, looked at the frontier woman and saw that "want, suffering, and boredom have changed her fragile frame but not broken down her courage." He noted that her children, "bursting with health, press around the woman. To see their strength and her weakness, one would say that she had drained herself to give them life and does not regret what they have cost her."

The market for farm products increased dramatically in urban

In this 1816 market scene, farm women bring their produce into the city to sell. Women in the expanding cities often had small gardens (or none at all) and depended on such markets to buy food for their families.

areas because city dwellers had less ability or need to produce farm goods themselves. Before 1800, town and city dwellers often kept poultry and livestock in their backyards or on the town commons, and they kept a well-stocked garden going as well. As cities grew, leading citizens worked to ban animals that had become health problems and nuisances. As land became more scarce and more expensive, the working class was forced into crowded tenement apartments.

Because of these changes, women in cities like Boston and New York were no longer making the farm products that their grandmothers had. But the new manufacturing technology had done little to transform life for most city women. For working-class women, the new cash economy made life harder and meaner. Then as now, women earned far less than men and were grouped into industries, such as textile, millinery (hat-making) and shoe-making, that were recognized as primarily "women's work." A New York charity reported in 1817, "The great disproportion which exists between the prices of labor of men and women is a matter of serious regret."

Most women wage workers in New York City labored in the clothing industry. In most cases they took "outwork"—sewing together pieces of cloth into whole garments in their own homes. Because of the cutthroat competition in the clothing trade, the prices paid for such work were very low. A woman could barely keep herself, let alone her dependent children, clothed, sheltered, and fed. Factory owners made these conditions worse by abruptly cutting prices, withholding pay, and inventing numerous other frauds to keep from paying women their due. Reformer Matthew Carey noted in 1830 that seamstresses had little recourse against such unscrupulous practices: "If the price of shirts were brought down to six cents they would accept it, and thankfully too. Their numbers and their wants are so great, and the competition so urgent, that they are wholly at the mercy of their employers."

For women whose husbands were working, such practices made life difficult but not impossible. As long as their husbands brought in a steady income, reductions in women's pay meant hardship, not necessarily starvation. The problem was that conditions for working men were not much better than for women. Although they were paid more than women, most working-class men brought in just enough money to provide the basics. Any unforeseen emergency, such as a medical problem, could send a family to the poorhouse. If the man was too sick to work, or injured on the job, the family could starve. With little access to medical care, and with abysmal working conditions, death was an ever-present possibility. Such protections as unemployment insurance, Social Security, and Medicare were a century away. Given these pressures on the head breadwinner, many a man abandoned his wife and children for a fresh start in another town. His family, meanwhile, was left with few ways to survive.

One option for single women that offered some degree of security was domestic work, but here they paid a price as well. Hours were long, longer even than factory work or outwork. Many domestics worked from five in the morning until ten at night, six and sometimes seven days a week. One man who had grown up being served by domestics remembered how difficult the work was:

> Oil lamps required trimming and filling; candlesticks . . . were to be cleaned; wood and coal to be brought from the cellar to all the fires . . . in all sitting rooms. All water required for the kitchen, or bedrooms, or for baths, was drawn from the nearest street pump, and all refuse water and slops were carried out to the street and emptied into the gutter. The street, for half its width in front of each building, was to be swept twice a week.

Domestics also were in charge of preparing three meals a day, as well as afternoon tea.

After 1800, elite society came to expect that "ladies" would refrain from menial chores around the house. One domestic writer

This illustration from an 1853 domestic guide shows a woman making pies while drying laundry by the fire and watching two children. Although advice from books and magazines helped women manage their housework and supervise their servants, it also created higher standards for housewives.

observed, "Women might work, but not ladies; or when the latter undertook it, they ceased to be such." There was thus an ever-widening gulf between mistress and servant during this period, and the domestic was made to understand this difference in rank.

The growing distance between mistress and domestic led to numerous tensions between the two. Advice about the home in the newly popular magazines written for women increasingly described the role of the lady of the house as being a manager. She was to ensure that those beneath her performed their duties exactly as she prescribed them. One Irish domestic, Rose Butler, complained that her mistress "was always finding fault with my work, and scolding me." Butler's response was to scatter hot coals outside the fire grate, in the hopes that her mistress's enraged response would be to send her back to Ireland. Instead the domestic managed to burn the house down, and was convicted of arson. Though not all domestic-mistress relationships ended in flames, there were certainly numerous emotional fires that burst out on both sides.

However, the job was not without its advantages to domestics. Because employers provided room and board as well as a small salary, a domestic had money for things other than the bare necessities. This surplus she often used to purchase the latest in "ready-made" fashions. The sporty dresses in turn gave domestics an entree into the giddy whirl of urban night life, in part making up for the drudgery of their jobs. Employers often were scandalized by such shows of fancy dress. Many mistresses believed a domestic servant should save her money to help her achieve eventual middle-class status. In various letters, mistresses decried the "outlandish hot looking dresses" of their employees, seeing these "crimson and scarlet shawls, ribbons, and faded bonnet flowers," backed by "sultry yellow calico," as an invitation to sin and sexual misconduct.

Many working women chafed against such tight supervision. They felt that while domestic work paid well, the job just wasn't worth it. Many women fell back on domestic work when all other options were unavailable. Some domestics even chose prostitution rather than submit to the orders of a mistress. Though opportunities for prostitution ranged from high-class hotel establishments to the lowest waterfront saloon side-rooms, all prostitutes were vulnerable to a wide range of sexual diseases. Those women plying their trade independently, or in the less genteel establishments, were especially vulnerable to violence by customers, proprietors, or criminals.

When working women chose prostitution over domestic service, they were rejecting in no uncertain terms the moral assumptions of middle-class America. It was a choice most mistresses explained away by pointing to the "natural" moral laxness of the poor. Certainly, upper-class women were not ready to admit that servants were so scarce because working conditions were so trying. Domestics became even more scarce in the 1820s, after the development of power mills in New England. These mills provided American women with their first opportunity at respectable, relatively safe work at reasonable wages.

The entrepreneurs who began the massive New England mills in Lowell, Waltham, and other mill towns sought to attract young, unmarried women as their primary workers. Owners believed these women would accept lower wages than men, particularly married men. At the same time, the owners could offer these women advantages that most other employers could not. Mill work offered women high wages in comparison to other jobs available to women, relative independence from their family, and a convivial group of like-minded young women. Most of the workers came from small farm towns in northern New England. Mill owners provided supervised boarding facilities that protected women workers from what the mill owners saw as temptation and sin. The location of the mills, set among rural villages, kept women sheltered from the lures of the city's bright lights. These conditions persuaded parents that mill work was an acceptable occupation for their daughters, at the same time that owners appealed to the young women themselves.

Farm women went to the mills for a number of reasons, which rarely had much to do with supporting their families. Mary Paul, a farm woman from Vermont, went to work at the mills when she was 15. Before quitting her job as a domestic servant, she wrote her father for permission to work at Lowell, explaining, "I think it would be much better for me in Lowell than to stay about here. I am in need of clothes which I cannot get about here." Sally Rice, another Vermont farm woman, explained to her family, "I am 19 years old. I must of course have something of my own before many years have passed over my head. And where is that something coming from if I

The mills of Lowell, Massachusetts, attracted young women from farming towns throughout New England. Mill work was considered respectable, and it paid better than domestic service.

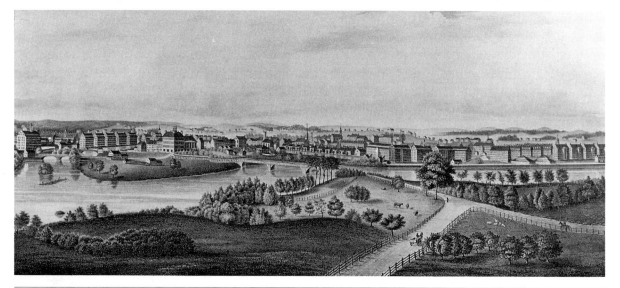

go home and earn nothing. You may think me unkind but how can you blame me for wanting to stay here. I have but one life to live and I want to enjoy myself as well as I can while I live."

Although these women were separated from their families, they were not without connections to home. Many followed sisters and cousins into the mills. Older relatives helped newcomers secure positions in the mills on arrival, and taught them the rules of both work and social life in the mill community. Families also expected older relatives to keep an eye on the newcomers.

These workers had come to expect a certain level of respect from both the outside world and the mill owners. Mill workers believed that they were in partnership with the owner—subordinate partners, to be sure, but nonetheless members of the company who were crucial to the success of the business. When the owners responded to increased competition and poor business conditions with sharp reductions in wages and increases in the rents they charged in their boardinghouses, many women workers were outraged. As conditions continued to decline during the 1840s, mill owners began to turn to recent immigrant women, such as the Irish, who would accept lower pay and more work.

The workers did not surrender without a fight, however. As owners shifted their policies from that of stern but benevolent father figures to cutthroat businessmen, many workers began to reject the rhetoric of the mill as a family. Instead, they used the sense of solidarity and

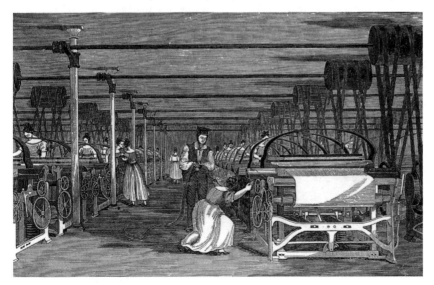

Women operate power looms to weave cloth in a factory. Before the introduction of the power loom, weaving by hand was an arduous task that had required the hard physical labor of men. Now, women could do the work and for lower wages.

The Merrimack mills in Massachusetts required their women workers to live in company boardinghouses. The constant supervision the company provided helped convince parents that mill work was a suitable occupation for their daughters.

worthiness gained from their work experience to create a movement that would fight for their rights. Their actions were part of a broader trend of women making their voices heard in the public arena.

Slave women, of course, had even less choice of jobs and working satisfaction. Their master or mistress usually determined which tasks they would perform. Women were sent to the fields just as men were, and they were expected to do their share of the work. Slaveholders cared little about preserving a "women's sphere" for field workers.

Cotton was surely king in the plantation South, and although some regions produced rice, tobacco, and sugar as well, most slaves' memory of work revolved around picking cotton. Slave women recalled the intense physical labor that such work required. As one former slave recalled in an interview (transcribed exactly as it was heard): "It don't make no difference if you big or little, you better keep up or the drivers burn you up with the whip, sure 'nough. 'Bout nine o'clock they hollers, 'cotton up' and that's the quittin' signal. We go to the quarters and just drop on the bunk and go to sleep with nothin' to eat."

Slaves were usually segregated into men's and women's gangs. Men tended to do jobs that required greater strength, such as plowing, while women were assigned to hoeing. However, there were a number of slave women who took to plowing, a job that demanded great skill as well as strength. Indeed, there were few jobs that slave women did not do, including planting seeds, digging ditches, making fences, and clearing new ground for planting. While women were

Most slaves, both women and men, worked in the fields. Slaveholders usually did not maintain the same distinctions between women's and men's work for their slaves that they did for whites. For example, women slaves shared the difficult tasks of digging ditches and planting crops.

often not expected to accomplish as much as men, a number of women slaves exceeded the output of their male counterparts. For these women, their work was a source of pride.

While some women attempted to make the best of an oppressive system by being productive workers, many others chose to do just enough to get by. These women were constantly feeling the sting of the overseers' or drivers' lash. Some women simply did not have the physical stamina to keep up the pace demanded by brutal supervisors, but were whipped all the same. Many slave women learned to feign illness to avoid work, often complaining of vague "female problems." While some of these complaints were no doubt valid, slave women knew that their reproductive organs had economic value to slaveholders, who were loathe to risk their slaves' ability to bear children.

A small percentage of the slave work force, about 5 to 10 percent, worked in the "Big House," as the plantation manor was called. Most of these workers were women, who labored as cooks or maids. The house slave was often accorded more status in the slave community, and often could pilfer some particularly tasty treat when the mistress was not looking. As one slave recalled, "House servants above the field servants, them days. If you didn't get better rations and things to eat in the house, it was your own fault."

Although house slaves like this cook had higher status than field slaves, they were under constant supervision of the plantation mistress and often were punished for not meeting her unrealistic demands.

Despite these advantages, many slave women preferred to work in the fields. In part, this was because of the demanding nature of the work. House slaves were responsible for all aspects of preparing the meals, from making sausage and jams to washing the dishes. Washing and ironing for the entire household was another constant, backbreaking task. House servants had to be at the mistress's beck and call at all hours. In addition, many mistresses set unrealistic standards for their domestics. Any wrinkle in the laundry, any dust speck on the mantle, might initiate a whipping by the mistress.

A few lucky women were trained as midwives, a skill that also provided status and a great deal of satisfaction. One ex-slave told of how when she was 13 "my ol' mistress put me with a doctor who learned me how to be a midwife. I stayed with that doctor for five years. I got to be good. Got to be so he's sit down and I'd do all the work. When I come home, I made lots of money for old miss. Lots of times, didn't sleep regular or get my meals on time for three, four days. 'Cause when they call, I always went. Brought as many white as colored children."

Slaves considered the tumble-down houses their masters gave them their homes, and women took pride in maintaining the places where they lived. Men, for their part, would repair the houses and build furniture. Black women and men struggled as best they could to maintain their dignity within the dehumanizing system of slavery.

White southern plantation women, while certainly benefiting from slave labor, also were responsible for much of the plantation's labor. Whereas the master hired an overseer to do much of the dirty work, the mistress was in effect the overseer of the Big House, including the tending of livestock and poultry and the production of food and clothing. Additionally, the mistress took on a number of tasks for which she did not trust her slaves. Even the most privileged mistress had to take on fairly strenuous tasks from time to time, such as processing the various by-products of slaughtered animals.

The mistress and the slaves she supervised shared their work space in constant tension. In some cases, mistresses used brute force, resorting to repeated whippings, and occasionally slaves responded in kind. But more often, slave and slaveholder were involved in an elaborate chess match with each other to determine how power would be divided in the Big House.

Not all southern whites and blacks lived on large plantations. Even though the industrial development of southern cities and towns lagged far behind the North, a significant minority of southerners lived in urban areas. Work for white women in towns was similar to that of their northern counterparts, minus some of the advantages of northern industrial buying power. Ready-made goods were more expensive and less available in the South, and most southern women continued to produce their own food and clothing from scratch.

Another significant section of the southern population lived on small holdings, where they worked their land without slaves. These were usually small farms run by a family, and life for women on these places was similar to that of women on the northern frontier—many children, backbreaking work from morning until bedtime, and not much chance to get ahead, unless one was willing to move to the frontiers of Arkansas or Texas.

In the North, privileged women could not force anyone to work as a domestic. Most middle-class women during this period either could not afford or could not find hired help. Even those women who were lucky enough to hire a servant found that there was still plenty of work to do. Although middle-class women no longer did much of the productive work of their foremothers, they found themselves working nearly as hard. While they had access to new technology, they often found that "labor-saving devices" saved the labor of men, but not of women.

Lewis Miller, a carpenter and popular sketch artist in York, Pennsylvania, drew this scene, which illustrates early 19th-century cooking methods. Before stoves were introduced, women would hang a pot of stew over a fire or put bread in a brick oven to bake while they did other chores.

COOKING STOVES.

With the introduction of the stove, domestic manuals and women's magazines offered elaborate new recipes to readers and pressured wives to produce more complicated dishes for their families.

The introduction of four-burner stoves by the mid-19th century is a good example. Cooking used to be a very straightforward procedure. A woman would hang an iron pot over a fireplace and cook one-pot meals for her family. But by mid-century, women's magazines and books insisted on new, more complicated, and time-consuming cooking techniques using the four-burner stove. Baking, for instance, had become a symbol of prestige for the women of the Northeast. Harriet Beecher Stowe and Catharine Beecher, who produced the foremost domestic manual of the period, asked rhetorically:

> Bread: What ought it to be? It should be light, sweet, and tender. This matter of lightness is the distinctive line between savage and civilized bread. The savage mixes simple flour and water into balls of paste, which he throws into boiling water. The air cells in bread thus prepared are coarse and uneven: the bread is as inferior in delicacy and nicety to that which is well kneaded as a raw servant to a perfectly educated lady.

All that stood between civilization and savagery, between the elite and the mob, was the respectable housewife's tireless effort to produce refined bread for her family.

Beecher and Stowe, like other domestic writers, hoped to establish housewifery as a respected occupation based on scientific techniques and a firm moral foundation. Beecher had led the way in these efforts with her pathbreaking *Treatise on Domestic Education,* first published in 1841.

Beecher believed that once housewives were properly trained, they could claim and exercise the power in the domestic realm that they were denied in the public one. Beecher had no patience with talk of women's suffrage or women's rights. She believed that women's inequality in relation to men helped contribute to "the general good of all." By gaining power over the home, however, Beecher declared that American women were "committed to the exalted privilege of extending over the world those blessed influences which are to renovate degraded man." The efficiently run, morally uplifted home would save the American republic from degradation.

Beecher's work built on the work of many domestic writers who had been advising middle-class women since the late 18th century. Sarah Josepha Hale, who edited *Godey's Lady's Book* from 1837 until her retirement in 1877, at the age of 90, was perhaps the most influential domestic writer of her time. By 1860, *Godey's* had broken all readership records with a subscription list of 150,000. Hale achieved these numbers with a philosophy that celebrated women in her sphere while disapproving of "this notion of female voting." The home, explained Hale, "was the sacred residence designed by divine goodness for her happiness."

By elevating women's work to the level of national purpose, domestic writers created both emotional and physical burdens for women. Yet by the late 19th century, women would use the ideal of the well-run, morally enlightened home as a model for the way the world should be run. By making the home morally superior to "the world"—men's sphere of politics and business—domestic writers were unwittingly providing future women with the means to press their case for the necessity of women's perspective in running the government. After all, why try to raise morally upright sons if only to see them abandoned to the vicious, amoral world outside the home?

The new emphasis on women's domestic skills had a more immediate impact on middle-class women's status. Catharine Beecher, Sarah Josepha Hale, and others supported the idea put forth by women reformers that girls needed to be broadly educated in order to take command of the home. The new woman of the 19th century, women educators argued, needed to be literate and thoughtful as well as skilled at traditional domestic tasks. Yet while early educational reformers stressed that women's education would complement women's work, some women would discover that education enabled them to rethink what type of work women should be doing.

As editor of Godey's Lady's Book, *Sarah Josepha Hale was an important figure for middle-class women. Hale celebrated domestic life and offered women advice on how to run a moral and efficient household.*

These hats and hairstyles—dubbed the "Latest English Head Dresses"—appeared in the January 1832 edition of Godey's Lady's Book.

CHAPTER 3

STEPPING STONES: WOMEN'S EDUCATION

I
n 1642, America's first woman poet of distinction, Anne
Bradstreet, sadly acknowledged:

> I am obnoxious to each carping tongue
> Who says, my hand a needle better fits
> A Poet's Pen, all scorn, I should thus wrong;
> For such despight they cast on female wits.

Many who lived during the colonial era believed that an overly
intelligent woman should indeed be despised, or at least feared.
Knowledge in a woman was a dangerous thing. Since women were
by nature irrational and emotional, men argued, giving a woman a
book was like giving a child a musket—she would not have the capacity to use it properly.

The idea of women's education began to emerge during the revolutionary era. Many social thinkers argued that a basic—though not
overly demanding—education was a prerequisite for any respectable republican mother. One popular textbook, *The American Pre-
ceptor*, insisted that Americans were "indebted to their mothers for
the seeds of virtue and knowledge." The book was quick to note,
however, that women's education would ensure "our daughters will
shine as bright constellations in the sphere where nature has placed
them." The ideal of the educated mother obviously took hold—in

*Seminary students in the early
1800s often engaged in a
strenuous course of education,
including geography, as
depicted in this scene done
with watercolor and ink on
silk. Many seminary students
would become teachers
themselves.*

Emma Willard, founder of the trailblazing Troy Female Seminary, insisted on women learning "male" subjects, such as anatomy. Always careful not to shock her wealthy patrons, however, Willard pasted paper over the images in the textbooks that depicted the human body.

New England, literacy among women went from 50 percent to nearly 100 percent between the revolution and 1840.

In the South, the situation was much less advanced. While reformers in New England were pushing for the establishment of mandatory public education, in the South leadership continued to depend largely on private schools. Thus only women from upper-class families received the benefits of education. Even fewer women slaves learned to read, because slaveholders viewed literacy as an invitation to revolt. Still, a small percentage of the slave population did learn to read, many of them taught by white playmates when they were young. Overall, few southern women were able to take advantage of the expanded vision that literacy and education offered.

At first, women's education in the North was meant simply to reinforce upper-class women's domestic talents. Subjects like French, English, and embroidery were especially featured at female academies around the turn of the century. By the 1810s, however, a new ideal of women's education was taking shape. While educational reformers still drew heavily from arguments about strengthening women's sphere, they now saw this sphere as necessarily including a knowledge of moral philosophy, literature, psychology, physiology, and a range of other subjects. The new women's seminaries that opened during this time sought to provide an education nearly equal to that of men.

In 1819, Emma Willard, one of the earliest proponents of expanded female education, argued for a state-supported system of female seminaries. In *An Address to the Public; Particularly to the Members of the Legislature of New York, Proposing a Plan for Improving Female Education,* Willard argued that her vision of an intellectually challenging education for women would bring about "a new and happy era in the history of her sex, and of her country, and of mankind." Although many legislators—and New York governor DeWitt Clinton—were favorably impressed with Willard's ideas, they were not willing to pay for them.

Willard did not win the legislature's support, but her pamphlet received warm reviews from the likes of John Adams and Thomas Jefferson. Having laid the groundwork for her plan, Willard turned to the town leaders of Troy, New York, to finance her dream. Troy's leading citizens, seeing Willard's school as an ideal opportunity for

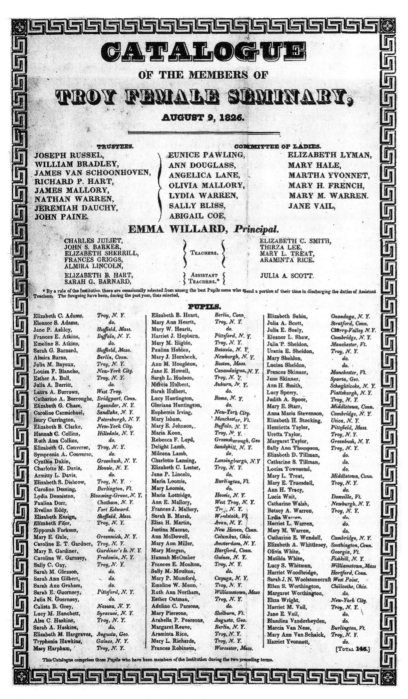

The 1826 roster of the trustees, faculty, and students of the Troy Female Seminary. Most of the 146 students came from upstate New York or New England.

their daughters, agreed to fund her.

Willard's Troy Female Seminary was the result of her 15 years of teaching experience and experiments. Her seminary provided privileged young women with the most demanding course of study available. One student reported that she had learned, "reading, writing, spelling, arithmetic, grammar, geography, history, maps, the globe, algebra, geometry, trigonometry, astronomy, natural philosophy, chemistry, botany, physiology, mineralogy, geology, and zoology"— and that was just for the morning classes!

Troy Seminary became a model for others to come, while Willard herself took to traveling the country as an advocate of women's education. In particular, she stressed the role seminaries could play in filling the growing demand for women teachers. Although women had started teaching as part-time replacements for men, New England school boards were quick to realize that they could be hired at half the cost of men—a fact Willard liked to emphasize. By 1850, Troy Seminary had produced more than 200 teachers.

Teaching proved to be an excellent opportunity for many young women. Although women teachers received only half of what men received, these jobs enabled single women to support themselves. The job also gave women more breathing space before getting married. Although marriage would most likely improve a woman's economic status, staying single—at least for a time—did not mean poverty.

For the entrepreneurially-minded woman, teaching could be transformed into a better-paying occupation. A number of women who had experience teaching chose to open female seminaries, or to take on administrative positions. Rachel Painter graduated from Westtown School, a Quaker institution in Pennsylvania, in 1812. She then taught at a Quaker school in Alexandria, Virginia, a position she loved. "I could not do very well without it," she wrote her family. "I have such a degree of infatuation in the pleasures it affords me that I should part with it with difficulty. I have the pleasure of seeing my girls improve so to fully answer my expectation." Teaching also had its monetary rewards. In 1817, she told an inquisitive cousin, "I can keep myself genteelly and lay up 300 dollars per annum, which brings me an interest of 8 per cent in bank stock." Eventually, she ended up buying a large share of the school herself.

Opening a school was sometimes the only way that a widowed woman could support herself and her children. Numerous middle- and upper-class women avoided almost certain poverty by following this course. Others, like Emma Willard, opened a school when their husband's business collapsed. Though Willard came to see her school as part of a crusade, it was also a business proposition. The tuition she charged was high, and Willard was able to prosper because of her able administration of the school.

Although Willard's Troy Seminary was a great success, only well-to-do women could afford it. Mary Lyon was responsible for bringing Willard's old idea for a publicly supported female seminary to fruition. Lyon envisioned "a residential seminary to be founded and sustained by the Christian public," with tuition and board to cost "as low as it may be." In order to keep costs low, train women in necessary skills, and improve discipline, the students themselves would perform the necessary domestic tasks. Lyon had experienced the problems associated with seminary boards of directors (who were usually all men). She therefore wanted her seminary to own its own property and to be self-supporting. By combining private contributions with local government support, she was able to raise enough money to build and sustain her project. In 1837 Mount Holyoke Female Seminary—later Mount Holyoke College—became the first endowed institution of female higher education in America.

Besides having a more diverse student body, Mount Holyoke differed from Troy in other ways. While Troy's curriculum had been broad, it had not been particularly deep. Lyon soon developed a four-year program of study, a first for women's seminaries. She instituted discussion classes about current political and social questions so that women could develop their own ideas. Mount Holyoke

Mary Lyon envisioned a seminary that would be inexpensive for students to attend, thereby allowing for a diverse student body. She founded Mount Holyoke Female Seminary in 1837.

This lithograph of Mount Holyoke Female Seminary was made from a drawing by Persis Goodale Thurston, who graduated from the school in 1845. Located in South Hadley, Massachusetts, the seminary later became Mount Holyoke College.

As a student at Mount Holyoke, Lucy Stone found that her ideas about women's rights and the abolition of slavery were unacceptable. She transferred to the more radical Oberlin College and graduated in 1847.

kept up with the latest scientific theories and provided its students with a small laboratory in which to pursue their own ideas. The school fulfilled Lyon's vision of a place for women to explore their own intellectual strivings.

Lyon died in 1849, at age 52, exhausted by her lifetime of work for the cause of women's education. Her legacy, however, was substantial. The success of Mount Holyoke ensured that the notion of a thinking woman would not be treated as an impossibility. Holyoke went on to produce even more teachers than Troy. Because of Mount Holyoke's advanced curriculum, many of its former students became seminary teachers themselves. And Mount Holyoke students, having spent four years of intellectual excitement together, created strong networks that they would draw on throughout their lives.

Despite Mount Holyoke's radical implications, it was still based on fairly conservative principles. Though Lyon hoped to expand women's sphere, she still believed that the ideal of separate spheres was fundamentally sound. And while she insisted on a woman's right to an equal education, her ideas about equality had limits. Thus when one of her students, Lucy Stone, persisted in distributing William Lloyd Garrison's fiery antislavery newspaper, the *Liberator*, Lyon made clear that such activities were not acceptable. Lyon found fighting for equality for white women was enough of a battle—she was not about to alienate her supporters by allowing the advocacy of racial equality.

Stone, who was to become a leading abolitionist and women's rights advocate, found a more congenial home at Oberlin College, in Ohio. Oberlin was founded in 1833 by radical antislavery activists—known as abolitionists—and Protestant evangelists. Oberlin accepted all qualified students, regardless of race or sex—the first such college in the United States.

At Oberlin, Stone met Antoinette Brown, and the two became allied in the cause to make the college live up to its radical intentions. Both thrived at Oberlin, but each found that their professors and fellow students were more comfortable with equality in the abstract than in the particular. Stone was kept from taking public speaking courses throughout her time there. Although the faculty recognized her abilities by granting her the responsibility for writing the graduation speech, she was not allowed to deliver it. When she discovered this conditional honor, she turned the opportunity down altogether. Despite these bumps in the road, she and Brown graduated together in 1847.

Brown, however, was not through. She hoped to continue her religious education and earn a doctorate in divinity from Oberlin. At first, the faculty was dumbfounded. No woman had ever made such a request, and the Oberlin professors found themselves once again having to explain away what appeared to be obvious hypocrisy. She later recalled, "I was reasoned with, pleaded with, and besought even with tears not to combat a beneficent order tending to promote harmony in the family and the commonwealth. Masculine headship everywhere was held to be indispensable to morality, and grounded in the inmost fitness of things."

Although Brown finally was allowed to proceed, the school ultimately backed out on its promise, and prevented her and another woman from receiving their degrees. Only in 1908 did the school grant Brown an honorary degree. Stone noted with irony that Brown "felt that she was commanded to preach, and to arrest the progress of thousands that were on the road to hell." Given these sentiments— so in keeping with the mainstream of Protestantism—Stone wanted to know "why, when she applied for ordination, they acted as though they had rather the whole world should go to hell, than that Antoinette Brown should be allowed to tell them how to keep out of it?"

Although Brown and Stone had to struggle to receive their due at Oberlin, at least the school made it possible for such a struggle

The diploma granted to Caroline Mary Rudd of Huntington, Connecticut, one of the first four women admitted to the full college course at Oberlin in 1837. Oberlin was the first college in the United States to admit all qualified students regardless of race or sex.

to take place. Despite its inconsistencies, Oberlin still offered unparalleled opportunity for women. Stone, in fact, became the first Massachusetts woman to earn a college degree. Stone and Brown would continue to support each other in the abolition and women's rights movements. They solidified their alliance by marrying into the same family—Brown married Samuel Blackwell, and Stone married his brother Henry. But although Brown became Antoinette Brown Blackwell, Stone insisted on keeping the name Lucy Stone, a unique claim at the time. No doubt many an old-fashioned critic looked at Lucy Stone and Antoinette Brown Blackwell as perfect examples of the harm higher education could do to two otherwise sensible women.

Thanks to the pioneering work of Troy Seminary, Mount Holyoke, Oberlin College, and other schools, when the first crop of American women writers and activists began to emerge in the 1840s, they were not universally looked upon as freaks. Instead, there was now a large core of women committed to intellectual pursuits in New England and throughout the North.

Indeed, some of the most prominent members of the transcendentalist movement were women. The transcendentalists sought to discover universal truths that would help one live a worthwhile life. Ralph Waldo Emerson and Henry David Thoreau remain the most famous names from this group, but women transcendentalists were important contributors as well.

Among the most celebrated were the Peabody sisters. Elizabeth Peabody was a leader of Christian transcendentalism and a publisher of transcendentalist tracts, including Thoreau's famous essay "On Civil Disobedience." Mary Peabody Mann collaborated with her husband, Horace Mann, on his research into educational reform. After his death, she coauthored numerous works on early childhood education with Elizabeth. Sophia Peabody Hawthorne, a writer and artist in her own right, contributed significantly to the work of her husband, Nathaniel Hawthorne.

Margaret Fuller was the most influential of the women who identified with transcendentalism. Fuller, in fact, brought together the group of intellectuals who swirled around Emerson by initiating a series of "Conversations," symposiums that touched on a vast array of topics. At first she offered the Conversations only to women, but she later opened them up to men as well. During 1839 and 1840 the

Margaret Fuller was a groundbreaking journalist and an influential member of the transcendentalist movement that flourished in New England. She proved that women could participate fully in the intellectual life of the nation.

Conversations were a center of intellectual activity in New England. In 1840 Fuller helped initiate and edit the influential transcendentalist journal, *The Dial*. She also participated in the transcendentalists' utopian community at Brook Farm, but chose not to live there. She wisely saw it for what it was—a wonderful place for a conversation, but a thoroughly impractical experiment in communal living.

In 1844, she began writing for Horace Greeley's influential *New York Tribune*. Greeley believed her to be "the most remarkable woman in America and in some respects the greatest woman whom America has yet known." Fuller became one of the first women columnists to move outside the domestic sphere, writing on everything from literary figures to prison reform to women's rights. In 1845, she published her groundbreaking work, *Woman in the Nineteenth Century,* which would influence numerous women's rights advocates in years to come. In it she argued, "We would have every arbitrary barrier thrown down. We would have every path laid open to Woman as freely as Man. As the friend of the Negro assumes that one man cannot by right hold another in bondage, so would the friend of Woman assume that Man cannot by right lay even well-meant restrictions on women." It was a heady call to arms.

Fuller reported for the *Tribune* in Europe between 1847 and 1850, another first for a woman. As she returned home on the ship *Elizabeth*, it seemed to many reformers in America that she was, as Greeley believed, without peer. But in the midst of a storm just a few hundred feet off New York harbor, the *Elizabeth* broke apart and then sank. Margaret Fuller's body was never found. She was 40 years old.

Although the words Fuller wrote would outlive her, perhaps the example of her life was her greatest legacy. Fuller proved that intellectual pursuits could be a woman's vocation. She demonstrated that a thorough education could equip a woman to achieve greatness. These lessons were a far cry from what early educational reformers had envisioned for women. Instead of planting women firmly in their sphere, education gave some women the tools to break through the restrictions society had placed on their potential. Critics of women's education had been right—too many ideas in a woman's head could be a dangerous thing.

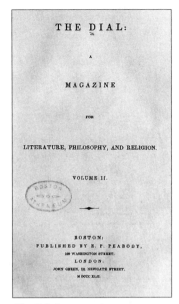

The Dial *was an important transcendentalist journal in which writings by Emerson and Thoreau, among others, often appeared. Margaret Fuller, who helped found and edit the journal, declared, "We would have every barrier thown down. We would have every path laid open to woman as to man."*

J.Cheney del. from R.Cosway R.A.   Pendleton's Lith

Devotion

A HIGHER VISION: RELIGIOUS ACTIVITY AND UTOPIAN COMMUNITIES

hen Lucy Stone was a young girl, she came upon the biblical command in Genesis, "Unto the woman [God] said, I will greatly multiply thy sorrow and thy conception; in sorrow thou shalt bring forth children; and thy desire shall be to thy husband, and he shall rule over thee." Stone closed the Bible and solemnly asked her mother the best way to take her life. Young Lucy explained that she wished to obey God's will, but could not live in a world where she had to submit to such an oppressive commandment. Her mother tried to console her, explaining that the Bible was quite clear in this regard—it was a woman's duty to obey her husband. Lucy took another lesson from this. "My mother always tried to submit. I never could," she later remembered. In time, she would learn Greek, Latin, and Hebrew in order to master the Bible in its original form and discover if "men had falsified the text" in translation.

In 1800, the United States was an overwhelmingly Protestant nation. After the 1820s, greater numbers of Catholics and Jews would immigrate to America and join scattered communities of their brethren in the New World, but even then Protestantism would dominate American life. Protestantism was hardly one unified religion, however. Great battles were fought in the early 19th century over whose

Prayer and religious faith were an important aspect of most women's lives in the 19th century, as this 1828 lithograph, "Devotion," indicates.

CHAPTER 4

In 1824 Charles Finney started a religious revival in New York State that attracted mostly women, who began to take a role in organizing the revivals and even preaching. Finney's tent was 100 feet in diameter and could seat 3,000 worshipers.

version of Christianity would triumph among Americans. Throughout this period, women provided most of the foot soldiers, and many of the officers, in these grand crusades to save the soul of the republic. Issues of women's proper place in these religious wars became battles in themselves, splitting numerous sects and forcing Americans to confront the contradiction between women's submission and women's moral duty.

The most electrifying religious crusade began in upper New York State in 1824. There, evangelist Charles Finney set off a spark of religious fervor that would soon transform American religion. Religious revivals were not new in America; they had most recently intensified around the turn of the century as Methodists, Baptists, Presbyterians, and Congregationalists, among others, vied to bring new members into their congregations. But Finney's crusade was different. His revivals swept through the small towns of upstate New York with such speed and intensity that the region was nicknamed the "Burned-over District." His crusade encouraged scores of people to reaffirm their faith in Jesus and be "born again."

He soon moved on to the bustling towns of Utica and Rochester, where he found young women and men especially open to his preaching. But he also noticed that women were taking a predominant role in organizing and participating in the revivals. In some towns, more than three-quarters of the converts were women. When Finney left the Burned-over District and took his crusade to New York City—where he was an instant success—he brought with him a commitment to increase the role of women in practicing and preaching religion.

Finney was a firm believer in the doctrine of perfectionism. He held that people were not predestined to sin or salvation, as the Calvinists had earlier claimed. Rather, they could free themselves of sin, and in turn free the world, through prayer and good works. Further, he believed holiness resided most prominently in the individual, and that a person's connection with God was more important than the words or actions of ministers.

This approach to religion had much to offer women who hoped to move beyond the confines of their appointed sphere while maintaining, like young Lucy Stone, their religious convictions. Finneyite Protestantism gave women a moral compass that was, in theory, not controlled by a minister or a husband, but by God. It was the woman's duty to read that compass correctly.

By the 1820s, women had established missionary societies throughout the North. The first of these was the Whitestone Female Charitable Organization, which soon branched out to encompass all of Oneida County, New York, renaming itself the Oneida Female Missionary Society in 1814. By this point, the group was supporting evangelical efforts in the newly expanding towns along the Erie Canal. By the time it changed its name to the Missionary Society of the Western District in 1817, it had more than 70 auxiliary organizations and was contributing over $1,000 a year to support ministries across the northern frontier.

Suddenly, the female missionaries were a force to be reckoned with in the religious community. Thousands of lapsed Christians and nonbelievers had been "reborn," thanks to the efforts of the Female Missionary Society.

Protestant ministers did not always look favorably on women taking active roles in their congregations. Most prominently, Cal-

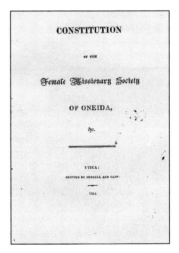

The Female Missionary Society of Oneida was one of several missionary groups that allowed women a larger role in religious life than previously. It spawned controversy in some denominations while gaining support in others.

The Oneida Institute of Science and Industry was founded in 1827 as a result of the intense religious revivals in upstate New York. It trained ministers for frontier missions and was one of the first colleges to admit black students.

vinists—the descendants of the first Puritan "pilgrims" who had settled New England—had once asserted that women were especially predisposed to sin. "Woman, Eve's progeny, by their naturally sensuous nature, have ever been Man's temptress," insisted one typical Calvinist tract. But as Eve's progeny filled ever more pews in the churches, even Calvinist ministers were recognizing "the selfless mothers and daughters" not as sinners but as saints.

Though most Protestant ministers encouraged women's role in religious life, the question remained just what that role would be. The Calvinist sects—Congregationalists and Presbyterians—were horrified at women speaking in public. Congregationalist minister Asahel Nettleton, who was a believer in emotionally restrained revivals led by ordained preachers, condemned those like Finney "who introduces the practice of females praying in promiscuous [that is, mixed male and female] assemblies." A Presbyterian association in New York objected to any participation by women in church services, arguing, "God has not made it [women's] duty to lead, but to be in silence."

Nonetheless, women did begin to preach. Perhaps the most influential woman preacher of the time was Phoebe Worrall Palmer, a Methodist lay minister who shared Finney's belief in immediate sanctification (the Christian belief in the state of grace that overcomes one upon acceptance of Christ as one's savior) and Christian perfectionism. Unlike Lucy Stone or Antoinette Brown Blackwell, who turned their evangelism toward equal rights activism, Palmer believed women should go no further than religious preaching. Perhaps because of her social conservatism, she was able to reach many people who were hostile to women's rights.

The Emmanuel Episcopal Church in Philadelphia. Women fill the pews in this scene, as they did in most Protestant churches, but church leaders usually did not allow women to become involved in church operations or preach to the congregation.

Born to an upper-middle-class family of 10 in New York City, Phoebe Worrall married a fellow Methodist, Walter Clark Palmer, in 1827. Each of the two times Palmer gave birth, the infant died within weeks. She and her husband took this as a sign from God that they should focus all their efforts on saving souls. Soon thereafter, both attained spiritual sanctification during a Charles Finney revival in New York City.

Palmer began her evangelical career with a weekly all-women prayer meeting she ran with her sister, Sarah Worrall Lankford, in their New York City home. In time, Palmer took on sole leadership of the meeting, which by the late 1830s had become known as the Tuesday Meeting for the Promotion of Holiness. In 1839, men were allowed to participate, and by 1840 the membership was so large that the meeting was forced to move to more spacious quarters. In later years, the meeting moved beyond its Methodist circle to include women and men from many evangelical Christian denominations.

Palmer gained even greater influence through her writings. While unwilling to support the cause of women's rights, she was adamant about women's rightful place in religious and charitable work. In *The Way of the Father* (1859), Palmer drew from biblical sources to refute conservatives' condemnation of women preachers, employing quotations such as Joel's prophecy from Acts 2:17, "And it shall come to pass in the last days, saith God, I will pour out of my Spirit upon all flesh; and your sons and your daughters shall prophesy."

In the popular book *The Way of Holiness* (1845), Palmer used her own life as an example of the quest for spiritual perfection and the opportunities women could find in spreading the gospel. She eventually published eight books and countless pamphlets, and in 1862 became editor in chief of the religious journal *Guide to Holiness*.

Many evangelicals were deeply involved in the antislavery movement, and none more so than the Finneyites and the Quakers. The basic tenets of the Quaker faith stressed egalitarianism (the belief that all persons, whether male or female, black or white, are equal before God and deserve equal protection under the law). Quakers had long encouraged women to speak their religious faith. Though some Quaker women were appointed lay ministers, most focused their attention on the monthly women's meeting. Quakers provided some of the earliest opportunities for girls to be educated along with boys. At the core of Quaker theology was the ideal of individual communication with God, deemphasizing the ministry. Quaker ministers were unpaid and were expected to facilitate prayer meetings

In a Quaker meeting, women were encouraged to speak out about their faith. The Quakers believed that all people are equal and that an individual's communication with God is more important than a minister's preachings.

rather than to direct a service. The women's meetings were led by women ministers.

By the 1820s, however, conservative Quakers were stressing the importance of the word of the Bible as interpreted by each church's Elders, who provided leadership and counsel for thier congregation. Since all the Elders were men, this policy tended to limit Quaker women's influence. In 1827, a group of Quakers called the Hicksites formed a separate group, rejecting the conservatives' growing drift away from egalitarianism and the individual's relationship with God. Named for their leader, Elias Hicks, they extended their egalitarianism to include the abolition of slavery. Whereas the conservative Quakers favored a gradual approach, the Hicksites joined with the more radical Finneyites to call for the immediate abolition of slavery.

Not surprisingly, the Hicksites tended to attract the most outspoken Quakers, including Lucretia Mott, one of the earliest American women's rights advocates. Mott learned her speaking skills at the Mothers' Meetings, monthly meetings for married Quaker women. When she was only 21, Quaker elders appointed her a lay minister. Mott credited the Quaker community with developing her views about women's role in society. "I grew up," she wrote, "so thoroughly imbued with women's rights that it was the most important question of my life from a very early day." Other Hicksites would join with Mott in the vanguard of the women's rights movement after 1848.

Christian perfectionism did not get very far in the plantation South. When the Finneyites and other evangelicals turned their social reform rhetoric on the evils of slavery, southern leaders demanded that their own churches toe the proslavery line or risk reprisals. The southern churches soon rejected the perfectionist and reformist agenda of their northern brethren. Perfectionism implied that society had to be vastly improved. Southern slavery apologists agreed with northern evangelicals up to a point—the northern cities were indeed swamps of iniquity badly in need of salvation. However, they viewed their own southern plantation society as beyond reproach. When southern religious figures did use Christianity as a means of reform, it was to chastise those few recalcitrant slave owners who went beyond the bounds of Christian decency in handling their slaves—those who tortured their slaves, for instance. Otherwise, southern churches came to realize that they could oppose slavery only at the risk of their livelihoods and even their lives, and they quickly fell in line.

At the same time, the church did provide solace, stability, and a woman-dominated membership for plantation women. Virginia Cary, writing in *Letters on the Female Character* (1831) on "the peculiar difficulties of our southern housewives," noted that "religion is at least most necessary to enable women to perform their allotted duties in life. The very nature of those duties demands the strength of Christian principle to ensure their correct and dignified performance; while the nature of female trials, requires all [the] power of

A slave women is weighed before being sold. Southern churches generally endorsed the slave system and did not use Christian teachings as a method of reform.

faith, to induce a requisite measure of patience and fortitude." In other words, religion enabled plantation mistresses to endure the atrocities of slave society with a modicum of inner peace.

Planters had mixed feelings about exposing their slaves to Christianity. Southern men believed that religion, carefully administered by white preachers, encouraged slaves to accept life as it was. The slave's reward could come in heaven, not on earth, white preachers claimed; the slaves would be assured of eternal salvation by their unceasing loyalty to their master. But Christianity offered the same subversive messages about moral standards, freedom, and individual empowerment to slaves as it did to northern white women. Not surprisingly, slaves were especially fond of the tale of Moses leading the Jews out of bondage from Egypt.

Some slave women used Christianity as a weapon of passive resistance against their owners. One old slave, having endured numer-

Some planters believed that allowing their slaves to attend church services would keep them loyal and humble. Often, however, slaves turned to religion to gain hope for freedom and moral superiority over their owners.

ous beatings, told her mistress one day, "I'm saved. Now I know the Lord will show me the way. I ain't going to grieve no more. No matter how much you all beat me and my children the Lord will show me the way. And some day we'll never be slaves." Since God was certainly morally superior to the master, and the individual slave was answerable in the end only to God, a slave's Christianity could undermine the master's authority.

Black religion kept the emotional quality and various myths and beliefs of West African folk religions, and was shared by the whole family, indeed by the entire community. Slaves would have thought little of the idea of religion as a woman's "natural" province. Slave women were not expected to be moral paragons or natural educators—qualities that society typically assigned to middle-class white women that made them "especially suited" to Christianity. Nor did slave women need Christianity as a means to fill up a feeling of uselessness—they were plenty busy as it was. Finally, black men were not off in a separate world of business—their work was rooted in their immediate and extended family, and their community.

Religion was a family affair for frontier families as well. Like black slaves, white men and women on the frontier did not make a sharp divide between work and home. There were rarely enough women in a frontier community to build the type of female religious network found in more settled areas. The camp meeting, an outdoor religious gathering, provided the type of community celebration that broke the monotony and isolation of frontier life. As an eastern newspaper reported, "A camp meeting [on the frontier] is the most mammoth picnic possible, as at a barbecue, the very heart and soul of hospitality and kindness is wide open and poured forth."

If evangelism ignited a spirit of community and kindliness toward one another, it could also unleash bigotry and intolerance. Evangelism was based on the belief that only those "born again" would make it into the kingdom of heaven. Nonbelievers could be saved, but only when they accepted Christ into their lives. As one young convert wrote in her diary, "He that is not with us said the Saviour is against us." Since the other side belonged to Satan, religious groups that did not conform to the broad expectations of mainstream Protestantism were often demonized. Both the Mormons and the Catholics found themselves cast as Satan's helpers just as

the evangelist tide crested in the 1830s.

Some of the most threatening attacks against Catholics were directed at nuns. Most of the nuns in the early 19th century were immigrants from Europe who came to America as missionaries. With their distinctive uniform, European manners and speech, and belief in a strict class hierarchy, many of these immigrant nuns suffered severe culture shock upon arrival in America.

Perhaps the worst attack on a convent occurred in 1834, when a mob sacked and burned the Ursuline convent in Charlestown, Massachusetts. Trouble began after a rumor spread that a nun, Elizabeth Harrison, was being held in the convent by force. Anonymous letters were sent to the convent warning the inhabitants that "the convent would be pulled down" if the "mysterious lady could not be seen." Even though five town council members searched the entire building and interviewed Harrison—who assured them she was under no compulsion to remain—a mob rushed the building with cries of "down with the convent." The mother superior, Mary Edmund St. George, was able to hide away the nuns and students. Unfortunately, she could not save any of the convent's sacred or valuable

This camp meeting had 456 tents staffed by more than 70 preachers, and drew a crowd of thousands. Camp meetings on the frontier were both religious and social occasions for families who often lived far apart from each other.

artifacts from the plundering of the mob. What the thieves left, the fire later consumed. During this period, anti-Catholic mobs burned down at least 10 convents.

Maryland was the most hospitable state for Catholics. The state contained a substantial Catholic minority, including many of Maryland's leading citizens. It was in Maryland that Elizabeth Ann Bayley Seton founded America's first Catholic order, the Sisters of Charity of St. Joseph. Mother Seton, born an Episcopalian, converted to Catholicism after her husband and her father died within several years of each other. Before converting, she had been active as a Protestant reformer in New York City. After coming to Baltimore to run a Catholic school for girls sponsored by St. Mary's College, she set out to raise funds for a religious community. In 1809, after securing the necessary funds from Samuel Sutherland Cooper, a recent convert, she established her convent near Emmitsburg,

This Massachusetts convent was burned in 1834 after rumors spread that a nun was being held there against her will. Catholics were often harassed because their beliefs and practices differed from those of mainstream Protestants.

Maryland. The order soon built communities in New York, Baltimore, and Philadelphia.

The Mormons had an even harder time gaining the acceptance of most Americans than did Catholics, in part because Mormons were intentionally attempting to create a society apart from the mainstream. Mormonism was established when Joseph Smith, an itinerant worker from upstate New York, published the Book of Mormon in 1830. Smith declared that he had translated long lost golden plates that contained prophesies from God. According to Smith, the plates instructed Americans to reestablish Christ's kingdom, which had once thrived in the New World. Mormons were to convert the Indians, who constituted the remnants of the lost tribe of Israel, and to follow the teachings of a new American prophet—Smith—to build a new Jerusalem.

Smith quickly attracted numerous followers, many of them rural and small-town people displaced by advancing industrialism who longed for a return to a more ordered world. Mormons believed in community cooperation and the sacrifice of individual success for the good of the community. Wherever they established their communities, however, they were harassed by distrustful neighbors and local governments. At one point, Smith even commanded a separate army in their colony of Nauvoo, Illinois. As tensions rose between Illinois officials and the Mormons, Smith began to search out possible havens for the Mormons in the West. Before the Mormons were able to emigrate, however, he and his brother were arrested for treason. On June 27, 1844, both men were killed by a mob led by many of the area's leading citizens. Soon after, the new Mormon leader, Brigham Young, led 12,000 Mormons westward to establish the state of Deseret in Utah.

In 1843, Smith had told his followers of a revelation he had received from God commanding the practice of polygamy—multiple marriages—for men. Although he attempted to keep polygamy secret, word of the practice soon leaked out to the non-Mormon world, and fueled much of the antagonism towards the Mormons. The careers of two of his wives illustrate both the potential and the problems for women under this policy.

Smith's first wife, Emma Hale Smith, married her husband in 1827 and endured years of poverty and hardship while helping to

Mother Elizabeth Seton converted to Catholicism and founded the Sisters of Charity of St. Joseph in Maryland. This was the first Catholic order established in the United States.

Joseph Smith, the founder of the Mormon church, was killed by a mob in Illinois before he could lead the Mormons into the West, where they hoped to find a safe area to settle.

build the newborn religion. Although she worked closely with her husband, acting as his secretary and editor, she was not chosen as one of the 11 witnesses to assent to the validity of the golden plates that contained the Book of Mormon. In a letter he wrote her soon after that event, Joseph Smith gently chastised his wife: "Thou art an elect lady whom I have called. Murmur not because of the things which thou hast not seen. Continue in the spirit of meekness and beware of pride. Let thy soul delight in thy husband." Emma Smith apparently assented to these sentiments. She soon established her own identity within the church, becoming president of its influential Female Relief Society.

In 1842, Joseph Smith described his wife as "the wife of my youth and the choice of my heart." Yet soon afterwards he took another wife in secret, and after his death the church established polygamy as official policy. After Joseph Smith died in 1844, however, Emma Smith denied that her husband had ever sanctioned polygamy. Choosing to remain in Nauvoo, she later helped establish the antipolygamous Reorganized Church of Latter Day Saints along with her son, Joseph Smith III. Although she later married a non-Mormon, she continued to profess the beliefs of the nonpolygamous Mormon church until her death.

Because of Emma Smith's hostility to the Utah Mormons, they bestowed the title of "The Mother of the Mormon church" on her rival, Eliza Snow Smith. Eliza Smith had lived as a companion to

Emma Smith and the governess to Emma's children before secretly marrying Joseph Smith in 1841. In 1849, following Joseph Smith's martyrdom, Eliza Smith became one of Brigham Young's wives. While in Nauvoo, Eliza Smith established many of the official duties for women within the Mormon church. As secretary of the Female Relief Society, she was its chief administrative officer; she later replaced Emma Smith as president.

Other religious sects began with the assumptions of women's heightened status. These sects—especially the Shakers—were searching for a purer spiritual and communal life. They were part of a widespread movement during the 19th century that rejected mainstream Protestantism and the new American industrial growth in order to create utopian communities in the countryside. All shared the notion that humans could create a more perfect world by separating from mainstream society.

Communitarians (those who lived and worked together in these idealistic communes) believed that two of the most basic problems with their society was the imbalance between women and men, and the inadequacy of isolated home life. Nothing was more harmful to a woman's soul, they thought, than to spend all hours of the day washing, ironing, cleaning, and raising her children. And men had no business going off to work away from the home, making money in some "unproductive" capacity such as a banker or a clerk. Instead, they believed, women and men should produce their foods and goods together and raise their children together. For some of these groups, these ideas led to nothing less than the reinvention of the family.

The Shakers, an offshoot of the Quakers, were founded in England by Ann Lee, a woman of humble background. Lee prophesied that the millennium, the new human order mentioned in the Bible that would arise shortly before the end of the world, had arrived, and that a new Christian church would be established in America. The first Shaker settlement, Mount Lebanon, was founded in upstate New York in 1792. By the 1840s, Shakers had established 18 societies in 7 states, including 4 in Massachusetts, 3 in New York, and 2 apiece in New Hampshire, Maine, and Kentucky.

Ann Lee's followers believed that she was Christ's spirit returned to earth, and that her female soul would balance out Christ's male

Emma Hale Smith, the first wife of Joseph Smith, did not accept the Mormon practice of polygamy and established the Reorganized Church of Latter Day Saints, which did not sanction the practice.

BRIGHAM YOUNG AND HIS WIVES.
COPYRIGHT 1898 BY THE JOHNSON CO., SALT LAKE CITY, UTAH.
INFRINGEMENTS WILL BE RIGIDLY PROSECUTED.

soul. They also believed that God was both male and female. True believers could only maintain the state of perfect grace made possible by Christ's second coming through "spiritualism, oral confession, community, peace, the gift of healing, physical health, the separation from the world," and celibacy (that is, refraining from sexual intercourse). In order to attain these goals, the Shakers did away with the idea of the nuclear family, with separate family units consisting of parents and their children.

A Shaker family consisted of from 40 to 80 people, related only by their commitment to their religion. Work was shared communally, as were the profits and property gained from the work. Although women and men in Shaker communities still worked in jobs traditionally associated with their sex, for women there was a great advantage to the communal work arrangement. The work was simply more fun when done in the company of others. Shakers usually sang, told stories, or had someone read newspapers and books aloud as they worked. In addition, the communal arrangement made for less work—it took five people much less time to prepare a meal for twenty than it did for five women to work alone preparing five separate meals for their families. The Shakers' system also saved money. Staple

Opposite: After Joseph Smith died, Brigham Young assumed leadership of the Mormon church and embraced the practice of polygamy. He is shown here with some of his wives, including Eliza Snow Smith Young (bottom right), the widow of Joseph Smith. Young is reputed to have had up to 27 wives.

Women prepare a meal in the communal kitchen in the Shaker village in Lebanon, New York. The women were instructed, "See that your victuals are prepared in good order and on time, so that when the brethren return from their labors in the fields they can bless you and eat their food with thankfulness."

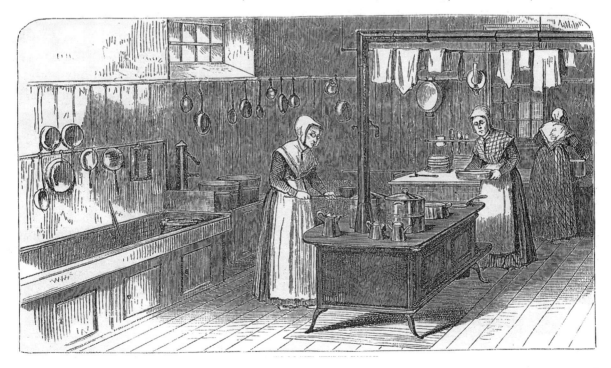

A Shaker meeting in the 1840s. Worship included whirling dances in which the Shakers expressed their religious fervor.

goods were cheaper when bought in bulk quantities, and communal kitchens required much less equipment than did groups of individual families.

The Shakers used their time well. They believed that frugality, industry, and cleanliness were basic to maintaining perfect spirituality. They used much of their free time to invent numerous items that made housework even easier. These inventions included an improved washing machine, a double rolling pin, the flat broom, a round oven for better cooking, a cheese press, an apple peeler—even the common clothespin. All served to save even more labor time for women. These activities also established women in a field for which they had rarely been given credit—as inventors.

The Shakers were able to convert their communal work system into profitable businesses. Communal kitchens had only to increase their work load a little bit to be able to maintain a restaurant. Since the Shakers had the means to process wool from shearing to spinning to weaving to dying to sewing, their clothes-making operation was extremely successful. Thus Shaker women were able to earn cash for their community and ensure its stability.

By the 1840s, American religious and utopian associations presented many American women with opportunities undreamed of at the start of the century. Although some religious and utopian ideas and practices called for women to remain in their traditional limited sphere, most provided women with a chance to redefine that sphere.

This washing machine was one of many inventions produced by the Shakers in their attempt to make housework easier. They believed that efficient work habits and tools helped them attain spiritual perfection; their motto was, "Hands to work and hearts to God."

Not all women living within America's boundaries were beneficiaries of these new opportunities, however. Indeed for many American Indian women, Protestant evangelism could become part of a threat to their way of life.

CHAPTER 5

CONQUERORS AND CONQUERED

Between 1800 and 1848, American settlers pushed westward in search of new lands. For the women who took part, the journey generally presented some hardship, some adventure, and the promise of new opportunities. American Indian and Hispanic women whose lands were being conquered, however, had little cause for celebration. For them, the appearance of the Americans meant that their way of life was about to take a dramatic turn for the worse. For them, expansion was invasion.

Since Americans now inhabited all the land between the Appalachian Mountains and the Atlantic Ocean, Indian tribes struggled to hold on to the lands between the Appalachians and the Mississippi River. As Americans pushed into Illinois, Ohio, Arkansas, the western Carolinas, and other border areas, the original inhabitants were often forced either to adopt white ways, or to be removed or annihilated by the U.S. Army.

The story of the Cherokee tribe illustrates how the lives of Indian people were drastically altered by American expansion. The Cherokees were one of the Five Civilized Tribes, so named because they had proved much more adept at integrating white culture into their own than had other tribes. In the eyes of white Americans, the Cherokees were perhaps the most "civilized" of the five. Many Chero-

A romantic view of the westward movement, in which mounted Indians placidly observe settlers crossing the plains. The hope for new land and new opportunities caused people to push further west, past the Rocky Mountains, during the first half of the 19th century.

kees embraced the efforts of Christian missionaries and accepted Christianity. After a Cherokee named Sequoyah developed a written language—most Indians communicated only through spoken words—the tribe produced a Cherokee-language Bible. In 1827, they wrote out a constitution modeled after that of the United States,

Cherokee Alphabet.

D $_a$	R $_e$	T $_i$	ℰ $_o$	O $_u$	i $_v$
S $_{ga}$ O $_{ka}$	F $_{ge}$	Y $_{gi}$	A $_{go}$	J $_{gu}$	E $_{gv}$
ℐ $_{ha}$	ℛ $_{he}$	ℐ $_{hi}$	F $_{ho}$	Γ $_{hu}$	Ꮔ $_{hv}$
W $_{la}$	ℓ $_{le}$	ℓ $_{li}$	G $_{lo}$	M $_{lu}$	ꭰ $_{lv}$
Ꮉ $_{ma}$	ℴ $_{me}$	H $_{mi}$	ℑ $_{mo}$	Y $_{mu}$	
Θ $_{na}$ ꮏ $_{hna}$ G $_{nah}$	Λ $_{ne}$	h $_{ni}$	Z $_{no}$	ꭴ $_{nu}$	O $_{nv}$
Ꮖ $_{qua}$	ꮙ $_{que}$	℘ $_{qui}$	V $_{quo}$	ꮛ $_{quu}$	ℰ $_{quv}$
Ꮂ $_{sa}$ ꮝ $_s$	4 $_{se}$	b $_{si}$	ꭲ $_{so}$	ꭶ $_{su}$	R $_{sv}$
Ꮮ $_{da}$ W $_{ta}$	S $_{de}$ ꭲ $_{te}$	ℐ $_{di}$ ℐ $_{ti}$	Λ $_{do}$	S $_{du}$	ℛ $_{dv}$
ꮞ $_{dla}$ ℒ $_{tla}$	L $_{tle}$	C $_{tli}$	ℋ $_{tlo}$	℘ $_{tlu}$	P $_{tlv}$
ℰ $_{tsa}$	V $_{tse}$	Ir $_{tsi}$	K $_{tso}$	J $_{tsu}$	C $_{tsv}$
G $_{wa}$	ℴ $_{we}$	Θ $_{wi}$	ℴ $_{wo}$	ℐ $_{wu}$	6 $_{wv}$
ꮼ $_{ya}$	B $_{ye}$	ꭵ $_{yi}$	ꮕ $_{yo}$	G $_{yu}$	B $_{yv}$

Sounds represented by Vowels

a, as *a* in *father*, or short as a in *rival*   o, as *aw* in *law*, or short as o in *not*.
e, as *a* in *hate*, or short as *e* in *met*   u, as *oo* in *fool*, or short as u in *pull*.
i, as *i* in *pique*, or short as i in *pit*   v, as *u* in *but*, nasalized.

Consonant Sounds

g nearly as in English, but approaching to k. d nearly as in English but approaching to t. h.k.l.m.n.q.s.t.w.y. as in English. Syllables beginning with g. except ꭶ have sometimes the power of k.A.S.ꭲ. are sometimes sounded to, tu, tv. and Syllables written with tl except Ꮮ sometimes vary to dl.

The Cherokee alphabet, invented by Sequoyah, gave the Cherokees a written language. The creation of an alphabet and adoption of other white customs convinced the whites that the Cherokees were a "civilized" tribe but did not save them from forced removal.

and a year later they began a newspaper, the *Cherokee Phoenix*.

Although the Cherokees were willing to adopt some Anglo-American traditions, they held on to other parts of their culture. Within Cherokee culture, women were responsible for almost all agricultural production. They worked the soil, seeded and weeded the land, harvested the results, collected the firewood, cooked the food, and processed the leftovers for winter. Cherokee women also made clothing, pottery, and baskets for use by the tribe and for trade. Cherokee men were responsible for hunting, fishing, and warfare.

White Americans who observed the tribe at work were generally appalled by what they saw. "The women seem to work without cease or rest," said one affronted missionary, "and the men do little except rest." The missionary was secure in the knowledge that it was "natural" only for women to work in the home and men in the primary, money-earning occupation. How could Cherokees become good Christians, he wondered, if they maintained such savage customs?

One missionary, who had spent a number of years among the tribe, saw things differently. "Though custom attached the heaviest part of the labor of the women, yet they were cheerful and voluntary in performing it. I have perceived nothing of that slavish, servile fear on the part of the women, so often spoken of." Cherokee women recognized that hunting was not simply sport, as most whites saw it. Rather, hunting provided an integral part of the tribe's diet,

George Catlin, an artist who lived among various Indian tribes, sketched these Cherokees. Some whites considered Cherokee men lazy because they spent their time hunting, a sport for whites, while the women of the tribe seemed to work ceaselessly at domestic and agricultural chores.

shelter, and clothing. A white American male might take an afternoon off to hunt, combining the pleasure of an afternoon in the countryside with an opportunity to vary the contents of his family's diet. Cherokee men hunted in large groups, usually for periods of a week or more, in order to ensure the tribe's survival.

While Cherokee women recognized the importance of the hunt, they also understood that their central role in the tribe's economy gave them a claim to power. Because Cherokee women controlled so much of the food production, they were able to take an active voice in tribal matters. They also took the lead in trade negotiations with white Americans, marketing their corn to the newcomers in exchange for manufactured goods.

For a Cherokee woman, power in the community meant more power in her marriage. After marriage, the husband would come to

This European woodcut shows Cherokee fishermen in a canoe. Although Cherokee women planted and harvested crops, they recognized the importance of the male hunting and fishing parties that provided food for the entire tribe.

live among his wife's relations. If the marriage ended in separation, the man was expected to return to his mother's house to live. Any children born during the marriage would remain in the mother's house and would be cared for by the mother's extended family. Any shuffling of marriage partners took place while the core extended family remained constant, thus giving children a safe harbor from the usual problems of "broken homes."

To missionaries and other reformers, such arrangements made no sense, and they struggled mightily to instill the ideals of European domesticity into the tribe. Reformers hoped that the Cherokees and other tribes would embrace the ideal of separate spheres, so that husbands worked in the fields, wives in the home, and both knew their place.

Indian reformers encouraged Cherokee men to take up farming by introducing them to the wonders of progressive American agriculture. The reformers brought in the latest farm implements and hybrid seeds and explained the use of livestock, which the Cherokees had never raised. Cherokee men were encouraged to grow cotton and flax so that Cherokee women could spend their time spinning rather than working in the fields.

While reformers were happy to see Cherokee women taking up spinning, they were disconcerted to find that women also embraced livestock raising and progressive farming. Cherokee women saw these

The Cherokee Female Seminary, modeled on Mount Holyoke Female Seminary, opened in 1851. White missionaries encouraged Cherokees to abandon their tribal customs and accept the idea of a nuclear family in which the husband worked in the fields and the wife worked inside the home.

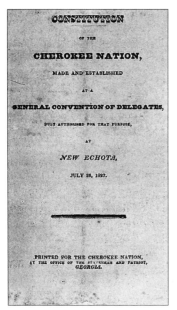

The Cherokee constitution of 1827 was modeled on the U.S. Constitution. But the state of Georgia nullified it in 1829 and forced the Indians to move out of the state.

tasks as the natural outgrowth of their traditional activities. Cherokee men, for their part, wanted nothing to do with such "women's work."

Missionaries then teamed up with a number of Cherokee leaders—women as well as men—to try to persuade the Cherokees to accept Anglo-American ideas about the roles of men and women. The leadership supported the establishment of schools, run by missionaries, that would teach young Cherokees about Anglo-American culture. Missionaries were especially concerned with "domesticating" Cherokee girls. One mission teacher wrote, "All the females need is a proper education to be qualified to fill any of the relations or stations of domestic life." The kitchen and nursery, not the fields, were the most important stations, "teaching industry and economy."

Although many ordinary Cherokees resisted these changes, the pressure from the outside and the example of some Cherokee leaders encouraged many of the tribe's elite families to convert to an Americanized way of life. For women, this meant a loss of power within the tribe and steadily eroded their independence and influence on tribal decisions. These leaders created laws that specified men were to control property during marriage, and that birthlines would be traced from the father, not the mother. In 1827, when Cherokees created their constitution, women were officially barred from voting on tribal matters.

Cherokee leaders had hoped that acculturation would lead to acceptance by whites. But while missionaries and reformers were concerned with the Cherokees' cultural transformation, most whites in the South merely wanted the tribe's land. These whites were supported by President Andrew Jackson, who had never hidden his prejudice against Indians. The state of Georgia nullified the Cherokee constitution in 1829 and demanded that the Cherokees sell their land to the state for $30,000.

Cherokee leaders, by now well versed in the ways of Americans, brought suit against the state of Georgia. Their rights of sovereignty were confirmed by the U.S. Supreme Court in 1831 (*Cherokee Nation* v. *Georgia*) and 1832 (*Worcester* v. *Georgia*). Unfortunately, Andrew Jackson cared as little for the Supreme Court as he did for Cherokees, and he effectively ignored these rulings. With the Indian Removal Act of 1830, Congress gave Jackson the power and the funding to institute a forced removal of the Five Civilized Tribes. In 1831, the Choctaw tribe was herded west in a forced march that would be duplicated by the other Civilized Tribes. This bitter journey to the Indian Territory (now Oklahoma and southern Kansas) became known as the Trail of Tears. Hundreds of tribal members perished from exposure, malnourishment, and exhaustion.

When most Cherokees refused to move in 1838, President Martin Van Buren—who had been Jackson's Vice President—ordered the army to round up those who resisted. The Cherokees, after being forced into detention camps, were then herded toward Indian Territory. More than a quarter of the Cherokee marchers perished along the way.

For Cherokee women, the ideal of domesticity did not bring peace and harmony, as the missionaries and Cherokee leaders had hoped. The ideal of domesticity had given northern middle-class women the opportunity to use the home as a jump-off point to political activity. For Cherokee women, however, domesticity meant the loss of their economic and political power.

On the Trail of Tears, more than a fourth of the Cherokees died from disease or exhaustion. The Cherokees fought their forced removal by suing the state of Georgia, and the Supreme Court ruled in favor of the tribe. President Andrew Jackson, however, refused to enforce the ruling, and the Indians were removed.

Narcissa Whitman and her husband journeyed to the Oregon Country and established a mission there for the Cayuse tribe. They hoped to teach the Indians about white customs and family life while also providing religious instruction.

Christian missionaries were not always so successful in converting American Indians to Christianity. The case of Narcissa Prentiss Whitman and her husband, Dr. Marcus Whitman, demonstrates this pattern. Without the support of the U.S. Army, Indian resistance to white missionaries could turn violent. The Whitmans were in the vanguard of the thousands of white settlers who would descend on the area known as Oregon Country (now the states of Oregon and Washington) in the 1840s and 1850s. Following what became known as the Oregon Trail, these settlers from the East leap-frogged the less hospitable Great Plains for the well-watered and forested coast of the Pacific Northwest.

While the overland emigrants came looking for new economic opportunities, the Whitmans and their party were more interested in saving souls. "I now offer myself to the American Board," wrote young Narcissa Prentiss, applying to the American Board of Foreign Missions in 1835, "to be employed in their service among the heathen." The American Board, which supported Protestant missions across the U.S. West and throughout the world, eventually underwrote the costs of the Whitmans' mission among the Cayuse Indians near Fort Walla Walla on the Columbia River.

While Dr. Whitman practiced medicine and taught farming techniques to Cayuse men, Narcissa Whitman ran the mission school and organized the output of the mission kitchen. The Whitmans were initially energized by the flurry of activities at the frontier mission. At first, they were able to witness daily progress. In a letter to relatives back East, Narcissa Whitman wrote, "We never had greater encouragement about the Indians than at the present time."

Once the missionaries began to settle into the routine of mission life, however, things began to unravel. After the Cayuse learned the basics of American agriculture and domestic economy from the Whitmans, they demonstrated markedly less interest in hearing about the saving grace of God.

Narcissa Whitman's life became a series of bitter disappointments. Her two-year-old child, Alice Clarissa, drowned. Whitman soon found herself the foster parent of 11 children whose own parents had perished along the Oregon Trail. Along with her many other duties, these new responsibilities exhausted her already depleted endurance. "My health has been so poor," she wrote her sister in

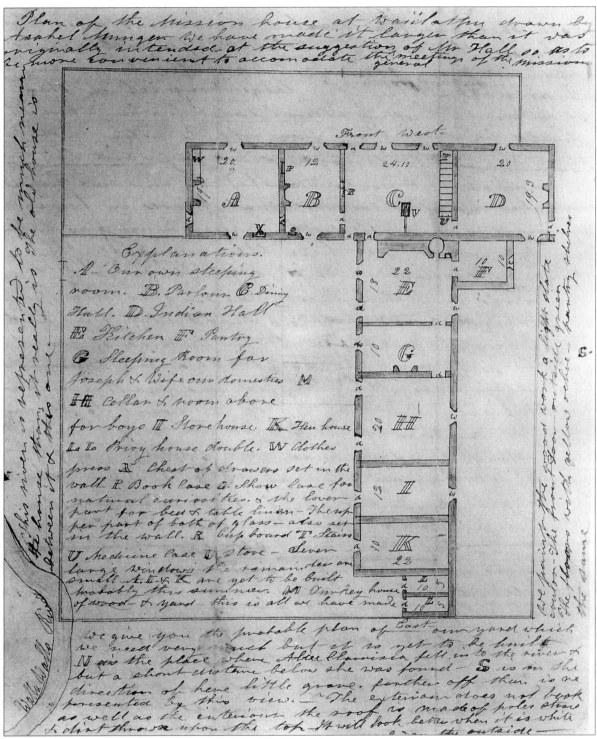

An 1840 letter from Narcissa Whitman describes the layout of the mission in Oregon. The Cayuse were initially eager to learn farming techniques and domestic tasks, but they were not interested in adopting Christianity.

1846, "and my family increased so rapidly, that it has been impossible. You will be astonished to know that we have eleven children in our family, and not one of them our own. Seven orphans were brought to our door in Oct., 1844, whose parents both died on the way to this country. Destitute and friendless, there was no other alternative—we must take them or they must perish."

Longing for the community of women she had left back East, Narcissa Whitman grew increasingly lonely at the frontier mission. After the missionaries' problems led the American Board to cancel support for the mission, Marcus Whitman went east for nearly a year to plead his case. Although he won continued support, his absence made Narcissa all the more miserable. By the early 1840s, the number of settlers passing through the mission increased markedly as "Oregon Fever" set in. Though the settlers provided Narcissa with more company, they also meant more work as the mission became an important way station for weary travelers.

The Whitmans had originally been quite taken by what they saw as the potential of the Cayuse to become "good Christians," but they soon changed their view. Narcissa Whitman increasingly saw the Indians as obstacles to white civilization and wondered if they would ever "progress" beyond "the thick darkness of heathenism." In a letter back East in 1840, she complained, "[The Cayuse] are so filthy they make a great deal of cleaning wherever they go, and this wears a woman out very fast. We must clean after them, for we have come to elevate them and not to suffer ourselves to sink down to their standards."

As more white settlers poured into the territory, the Cayuse and other tribes began to view the Whitmans not as deliverers of useful knowledge, but as harbingers of disaster. Narcissa noted the Indians' concern about the newcomers but seemed unaware of any imminent danger. "The poor Indians are amazed at the overwhelming numbers of Americans coming into the territory," she wrote in July 1847. "They seem not to know what to make of it." Once again, however, Whitman seems to have underestimated the Cayuse—they did indeed know what to make of the influx. When a measles outbreak—brought by white settlers—ravaged the Indian children while sparing the whites, the Cayuse blamed the Whitmans. The Cayuse believed that the Whitmans were now turning to witchcraft to destroy their tribe. They were not aware that the measles had spared many whites because they had the necessary antibodies, whereas the Indian children had no such protection against the unfamiliar disease. The Cayuse had already made the connection between the Whitmans' presence and the whites' invasion, and so were convinced of the missionaries' ill intent. On November 29, 1947, a Cayuse war party attacked the mission settlement, killing 14—including the Whitmans—and taking 47 prisoners.

Eastern missionaries mourned the loss of their martyrs, while eastern newspapers used the Cayuse as a clear example to argue that the rifle, and not the cross, would best "convert" the Indians. Another assessment was reached by a fellow western missionary, H. K. W. Perkins, who wrote:

> That [Narcissa Whitman] felt a deep interest in the welfare of the natives, no one who was at all acquainted with her could doubt. But the affection was manifested under a false view of Indian character. Her carriage toward them was always haughty. It was the common remark among them that Mrs. Whitman was "very proud." It was her misfortune, not her fault. She was adapted to a different destiny. She wanted something exalted—communion with mind. She loved company, society, and excitement. The self-denial that took her away from it was suicidal. She was not a

This print graphically portrays the murder of Marcus Whitman by a Cayuse Indian. A Cayuse war party attacked the mission and killed 14 settlers, including the Whitmans.

missionary but a woman, a highly gifted, polished American lady. And so she died.

The Indians of California were first conquered not by Americans, but by Hispanics from the Spanish colony of Mexico. These *Californos,* as the Spanish came to be called, were eager to convert the local Indian tribes to the Catholic faith. Unlike the American missionaries, however, the Californos established elaborate missions for the purpose of utilizing Indian labor while at the same time teaching Catholic beliefs.

The mission system called for Indians to pledge their souls to Catholicism, and to hand over control of their lives to the Catholic padres, or fathers, who led the missions. After a number of years of training, and vigorous tests to prove that these converted Catholics had been civilized, the transformed Indians would be freed from the mission's control and given their own land. They could then become independent small farmers and loyal subjects of Spain.

Like most missionaries' visions, the Californos' system was fatally flawed. Few Indians seemed to have become sufficiently civilized in the eyes of the padres to be released from the missions. Further, mission Indians were sometimes cruelly abused by the padres and the Californo soldiers. Once the Indians committed themselves to the care of the missions, they were not allowed to leave voluntarily; those who ran away were brought back in irons by the soldiers.

Spanish missionaries from Mexico worked to convert the Indians in California to Catholicism while forcing the Indians to work in the fields and perform other tasks at the missions.

Often, the soldiers would capture Indians who had never pledged themselves to Catholicism, who would then be forced to convert and remain at the mission. Although the converts were forced to work long hours in the fields and at various income-producing tasks, they received only food, shelter, and clothing in return for their work.

When the Spanish first appeared in California in the 1770s, many Indians thought them to be godlike creatures—they wore shiny armor, rode horses, and fired muskets—things that the Indians had never seen before. Many Indians thus accepted Christianity because they believed the Spanish to be more powerful gods than those worshiped by the Indians. In time, however, Indians came to know the Californos as men, although extremely powerful men, and were less

A Swedish visitor made this rough sketch of a mission kitchen/dining room in California. Although mission Indians maintained some traditional tasks like making tortillas, mission officials worked to force Indians to adopt Spanish culture.

inclined to join the missions, especially after they heard of the harsh conditions there.

In order to attract new converts to the missions, the padres specifically recruited Indian women. The missions had a number of advantages to offer them. Unlike many other Indian cultures, California Indian tribes were extremely patriarchal—power belonged to the men; women had little control either over the community's affairs or within their families. Thus the material conditions at the missions were much improved for women. As Father President Lausén, head of the Santa Barbara mission during the late 18th century, noted, Indian women in the mission had access to "grinding-stones, pans, pots, stew-pots, and even small ovens for baking bread." Indian men, whose job within the tribe was to fight and hunt, saw no such advantage in mission life.

The California missions had an even harder time attracting recruits after 1790. By that time, even Indian women were disenchanted with mission life. After 1800, the missions abandoned recruitment for outright coercion. Califorrno soldiers swept through the outlying areas and rounded up any Indians that could be found.

Although the soldiers were ultimately responsible for the destruction of the California Indians, their chief weapons were not the sword and the gun. Rather, the soldiers decimated the Indian population by spreading syphilis among them. This deadly sexually transmitted disease had been unknown to California Indians before the arrival of the Spaniards, and it wreaked havoc among the native population. The Spaniards most often infected Indians by raping Indian women caught in raids. Although the padres attempted to enforce laws against such violence within the missions, there was little they could do outside the mission walls.

The lives of mission Indians became even more difficult after the Mexican Revolution in 1821. After Mexico freed itself from Spain, its leaders were determined to free the new republic from the influence of the church as well. The new government ordered the missions to be privatized, and their land divided among mission Indians and Californos. Unfortunately, the Indians saw little of their promised lands; as a result many took to raiding Califorrno towns, while others took work as laborers where "all in reality are slaves."

The republic of Mexico did not have much time to profit from

their conquest, however. By the 1830s, a steady stream of "Yankees"—American entrepreneurs from the Northeast—were taking control of the territory's economic system. At first, the American presence seemed to offer much hope to the Californos. Most of the leading Yankees who established themselves in California sought to marry upper-class Californo brides. Within Californo culture, fathers had authority over who their daughters would marry. Most well-placed Califórnos readily consented to these matches. They were willing to relinquish their daughters and a percentage of land as a dowry (a wedding offering from the bride's family to the groom)—both of which they viewed as their property—in order to gain the status for their families associated with these wealthy newcomers.

By the 1840s, however, a new wave of Americans rolled in from the East who were unconcerned with integrating themselves into Californo society. Indeed, these Americans viewed Califórnos as lazy barbarians—much as the original Califórnos had viewed the Indians. They saw Californo women not as prospective marriage partners but simply as another feature of the conquered landscape. For Califórnos, that landscape had changed markedly—the conquerors were now the conquered.

An Indian woman in California uses a stone roller and slab to grind corn for tortillas.

A fur trapper with his Indian bride. According to artist Alfred Jacob Miller, he paid her father $600 worth of various goods, including guns, horse blankets, alcohol, sugar, tobacco, and beads.

Not all Americans who headed west acted as conquerors. Numerous alliances between fur traders and Indians were often struck up to help both sides succeed in the fur trade. Particularly noteworthy were the many liaisons between white trappers and Indian women, many of which ended in marriage. Often, these relationships demonstrated the potential for cross-cultural cooperation.

White fur traders who operated in the Great Northwest during the 19th century were little concerned with the niceties of Anglo-American society they had left behind. Indeed, white writers back East often grouped fur traders with Indians, calling them "barbarians" and "half-savages." Rather than being appalled at Indian women's ability to take on heavy labor, fur traders appreciated their services. As one Indian chief advised a trader, "One woman can haul as much as two men can."

Besides the ability to contribute her share of work, an Indian woman could also serve as a guide and translator. Hundreds of Indian women worked in this capacity for fur traders. Indeed, much of the trade would have been impossible for whites without the aid of these women. Some Indian women were hired by traders; others became romantically or sexually involved with them. In some cases, the women were exploited for their services and their sexual companionship and then abandoned. But in the majority of marriages, fur traders and their Indian brides maintained long-term relationships. Adopting the Indian custom, many of these men chose to live with their wife's family within the tribe.

White fur traders who took both an Indian bride and an Indian way of life were known at the time as "squawmen." Among whites, the term was meant to be derogatory, a sure indication that a man had buckled under to his wife's wishes. Among Indians, however, the label was simply a way of recognizing the man's choice to align himself with the tribe by accepting his wife's culture.

By the 1840s, as hunters depleted the numbers of fur-bearing animals that had once seemed inexhaustible, and settlers destroyed the animals' habitat, the fur trade receded to the far north. The mixed-blood culture of Indians and whites—the métis, as the French called them—survived within some Indian tribes, but remained largely invisible to mainstream American culture. Yet métis culture reminds us that cultural interaction need not always be a tale of conquerors and conquered, but rather a story of negotiation and understanding.

Captain Walker, a trapper, rides ahead of his Indian wife. An Indian wife was often a useful companion because she could serve as a guide and translator.

CHAPTER 6

STEPPING OUT: WOMEN IN PUBLIC

I sabella Marshall Graham awoke one day in 1773 to find herself a widow. The day before she had been married to a Scot-
tish physician, Dr. John Graham; the next day she was alone
with five young children, nearly penniless, and with few means
of producing an income. Despite these obstacles, she managed not
only to survive, but to prosper. For the next 20 years, she did quite
well as an educational entrepreneur, running successful schools for
upper-class young women in Scotland and New York.

In 1797, Graham joined with Elizabeth Seton—who had not yet
been converted to Catholicism—to found the Society for the Relief
of Poor Widows with Small Children. Charitable organizations for
poor widows had existed before—the well-to-do considered these
women to be "deserving poor," and therefore the proper objects of
pity. What was unusual was that Graham and Seton's organization
was among the first to be founded and run by women.

Graham and Seton were now in charge of an organization, running meetings, raising money, and lobbying politicians, tasks that
might have been considered inappropriate by the more conservative
elements of society. But these utterly respectable ladies were careful
to justify their efforts by saying that this type of work fell within the
proper sphere for women.

*In this Currier & Ives print, a
woman temperance crusader
smashes barrels of alcohol.
Reform organizations were
one way for women to enter
public life and bring about
social change.*

In 1797 Isabella Graham helped found the first charitable organization run by women. The organization offered aid to poor widows with children, which had been Graham's position when her husband died 24 years earlier.

A few observant folks realized that something was amiss with these benevolent societies, despite the respectable women and their careful language stressing "women's work." Conservative clergymen in particular remained uneasy with women's involvement in public matters. In 1815, Reverend Moses Stuart lectured the Salem Female Charitable Society that women's fundraising efforts had to be supervised by "men who are skilled in such matters." One year later, another minister told a New York City charitable organization that women should not "set themselves up as public teachers, . . . and so usurp the authority over man." The reverend did allow that it was permissible for "a few females assembled in private . . . to meet together for prayer."

Philanthropic women—those involved in giving to help the poor or needy—were not about to retreat, however. In many ways, benevolent women were among the most conservative members of society, whatever certain ministers might have thought. Benevolent women believed they were obligated, as Christians and as members of the elite, to protect those who could not protect themselves. How were these women to know that their first careful steps into the public arena would help other women justify activities such as debating political issues, gathering petitions to send to Congress, and organizing strikes? But just as changes in work, education, and religion could lead to unexpected opportunities for women, so too could the most innocent involvement in public affairs present women with new possibilities.

Isabella Graham and other pioneer philanthropists were first moved to act by very real problems. Poverty was on the rise in most American cities. Well-to-do women in New York, Boston, and other cities, watching poverty's steady advance, felt compelled to minister to the growing number of poor people around them. Seeing a need was one thing, but only the determined actions of a few strong leaders could convert opportunity into reality. Leaders like Graham and Seton encouraged women to take their first steps out of the domestic realm, and engage in various administrative tasks within the safety of the benevolent societies.

Benevolent women believed that they could no more hope to eradicate the causes of poverty than to banish death. By the late 1820s, evangelical women, led by the Finneyites, were challenging this pessimism. Evangelical women believed the poor could be up-lifted. In the view of evangelical reformers, immorality—not low wages, not misfortune—caused poverty. Rather than protect the worthy poor, evangelical reformers meant to make the poor worthy.

The Second Great Awakening, culminating in Finney's revivals, had electrified many middle-class women into action. A number of these women were recent graduates of the new female seminaries—they had a sense both of mission and of solidarity with other women. The attention of evangelical women was soon riveted on the plight of their less fortunate sisters, prostitutes and other "fallen women." In 1831, John MacDowell, a recent convert of Charles Finney, is-sued a report on the sordid business of prostitution in New York City. The report was thoroughly denounced by business leaders and politicians who feared it would give New York a bad name. Many women, however, were drawn to MacDowell's call to "virtuous women of the city . . . to employ all the peculiar influences of your sex in

Prostitution was one target of reform organizations. Christian women inspired to action by religious revivals felt it was their duty to help save these "fallen women" from the immoral men who were their customers.

promoting an Institution which is founded for the relief of the miserable of your sex exclusively." In response to this plea, evangelical women founded the New York Female Moral Reform Society in 1834. Six years later, the American Female Moral Reform Society (AFMRS) had 555 local chapters.

At first, the AFMRS sought to save prostitutes by getting them to renounce sin and embrace Christ. Reformers soon realized, however, that the prostitutes had customers, and that many of the customers had wives. Moral reformers asserted that a double standard existed: "Why should a female be trodden underfoot, and spurned from society . . . if she but fall into sin, while common consent allows the male to habituate himself to this vice, and treats him as not guilty?" asked the all-woman editorial board of the AFMRS paper, *Advocate of Moral Reform.* "Whence has this perversion in truth arisen?" For the women of the AFMRS, the onus lay with "the harder sex."

The Boston chapter of the AFMRS explained in 1838 that it was the society's duty "to guard our sisters, daughters, and female acquaintances from the delusive arts of corrupt and unprincipled men." In order to fulfill this duty, the New York FMRS took another step into the public realm—it spearheaded a petition drive to pass a state law making a man's seduction of a woman illegal. After presenting thousands of signatures to the legislature over several years, women reformers—with support of male allies—finally won passage of an antiseduction bill in 1848. Although the law was rarely enforced, the campaign proved that organized women could make the legislature to pay attention.

Custom had long granted women the freedom to petition the legislature. In the past, however, individual women presented petitions concerning personal matters such as divorces or contested wills. Once again, women were taking accepted behavior and stretching it to fit their needs.

Even the male allies of evangelical women felt that men were better suited to address indelicate issues such as prostitution. The men of the newly founded Seventh Commandment Society ("Thou shalt not commit adultery") gently suggested that the AFMRS could now retire to more "appropriate" endeavors. The New York FMRS quickly let their evangelical brethren know that only women could truly understand the problem. "This is the appropriate work for *women,*" a rural reformer insisted, "Go on, ladies, go on, in the strength of the Lord."

The AFMRS's activities brought women together as never before. Their efforts gave women reformers an understanding of their potential power as a group. Although most women in the AFMRS came from the middle classes, the society connected women from farms, villages, and cities. Local chapters learned the importance of "assembling *women* in general convention meeting," as the *Advocate* put it, at least once a year. These conventions, said the *Advocate*, brought to women "a clearer discernment of the capabilities of [women's] mental powers . . . which have been for ages . . . *lost to the world. . . .* It indicates an increasing recognition of . . .the *glorious*, the *heroic* bursting of *iron limits. . . .* When I regard the influence which they will exert in raising woman from the lowly path in which she has hitherto walked . . . I experience sensations of peculiar joy; *for I am a woman.*"

The newfound solidarity of women reformers enabled them to perceive a common enemy—immoral men. Not only were men the seducers, the philanderers, but they were also responsible for sustaining an economic system that perpetuated women's poverty. Many women reformers came to realize that the same system that consigned working-class women to low-paying, unskilled jobs also restricted middle-class women's opportunities. The *Advocate* protested in 1846, "Men have monopolized almost every field of labor. They have taken . . . almost every place where skill and talent is required, and they have excluded women." Prostitutes were simply poor women with no other recourse to survive. Only the continued health, sobriety, and business acumen of reformers' husbands kept most middle-class women from facing such a fate.

Evangelicals—women and men—were also involved in a tenacious struggle to shape the social mores and spiritual needs of the expanding middle class. The Burned-over District proved fertile ground for the same perfectionist fervors that had fueled the revivals. Rather than saving souls, moral reformers now intended to battle sin head-on; to eradicate temptation forever.

Reformers sought to become chaperones to the growing population of footloose, upwardly mobile men who came to the boom towns in search of new opportunities. Women reformers began

monitoring drinking habits, and they soon decided that total abstinence (that is, not drinking at all) was in order; they observed courting behavior and began ostracizing those who sought to "take advantage" of a young woman. Reformers pushed for stronger
Sabbatarian laws, insisting that church and not the dance hall or the
saloon should be the proper gathering place on Sunday. And they
looked askance at the young men's fraternal clubs.

Needless to say, many of the objects of the reformers' relentless
campaign were not overjoyed to be singled out for redemption. The
reformers' vision of "proper" middle-class life had become so domi-

*The Tree of Temperance bears
fruit in the form of "Hon-
esty," "Riches," and "Good
Children," among other
things. Reformers attacked
alcoholism not as a disease but
as an immoral activity that
was incompatible with a
respectable life.*

nant, however, that many men—young and old—who sought respectability did not fight women's right to enforce moral codes. Instead, these men joined in their own efforts to "live the goodly life." The most successful of these efforts—at least in terms of membership—were the temperance societies.

During the 1820s and 1830s, organizations such as the New York City Temperance Society (NYCTS) were concerned largely with maintaining the boundaries between the "laboring classes" and the "respectable classes." Membership in the NYCTS was both a mark of class distinction and an opportunity to make valuable connections. Following the Panic of 1837, fortunes both newly made and well established were shattered. The temperance movement that grew out of the wreckage embraced a new understanding of economic mobility, both upward and downward. The new movement, particularly the Washingtonian Society, founded in 1840, eagerly embraced redemption. Washingtonians welcomed the admitted sinner and supported his conversion to abstinence. This approach fit perfectly the perspective of evangelical women reformers.

Women began their involvement with the Washingtonians by establishing ladies' auxiliaries. At first, women were content to cook dinners for benefits and gatherings, organize social functions, and boycott grocers who sold alcohol. However, a group of more ambitious women soon established separate Martha Washington Societies, which began to focus more on the problem of men who had no interest in being redeemed.

Women's temperance societies had their own particular strate-

The emblem of the Boston Young Men's Total Abstinence Society. Many middle-class men approved of women's efforts to enforce temperance and considered sobriety a mark of distinction.

gies to gain young men's compliance with abstinence. As the *Massachusetts Cataract* explained, "When any of the tee-total ladies of these associations gives a social evening party at her house, it *happens* that those young nice men who refuse to sign the pledge, . . . and whose affection for the *bottle* is greater than their regard for the *belles* of those places, . . . don't get an invitation!" Martha Washingtonians used their position as organizers of social events to coerce men into accepting women reformers' notions of proper behavior. Like other women reformers, they accepted the ideal of domesticity, while pushing out the edges to make room for their expanded role in the public realm.

Not all women reformers saw themselves at a distance from the poor. In 1818, 30 women met in Salem, Massachusetts, to organize a moral reform society. Rather than attempting to improve the lives of another class, they sought to improve themselves. "We resolve to be charitably watchful over each other," they promised in their charter, "to advise caution and admonish where we judge there is an occasion, and that it may be useful; and we promise not to resent but kindly receive such friendly advise from our members." The society recognized the importance of building trust among its members: "We promise not to divulge or ridicule the supposed infirmities of any fellow member." The society pledged to provide mutual aid to each other during hard times and personal crises. After approving a con-

This lithograph, entitled "The Progress of Intemperance," depicts the plight of an expectant mother and her children abandoned by their alcoholic husband/father.

stitution, the Colored Female Religious and Moral Society of Salem was officially initiated.

This society was different not simply because it consisted of African-American women, but because it practiced mutual aid and mutual improvement. The Salem society was one of many such black women's societies created during the first half of the 19th century. Because the black upper classes were not far removed from the black poor—a steady job at decent wages constituted an elite—black societies were less likely to make class distinctions. Nor did blacks make distinctions between the "worthy" and "unworthy" poor. African-American women realized that racism helped make poverty a way of life for blacks.

By the 1830s, African-American women's societies had added temperance, moral reform, and missionary activities to their agenda. These groups included the Women's African Benevolent Society of Newport, Rhode Island, and the Female Benevolent Society of Philadelphia. Black women were also the first to initiate literary societies. Within an all-woman milieu, members met to discuss "improving literature." For most black women, such societies were the only means of intellectual development. Although the new seminary movement provided wonderful opportunities for middle-class white women, none of these institutions accepted blacks. Few black women would have had the necessary means to attend even if racism had not barred them. Early on, African-American women realized that only they could uplift themselves.

By the mid-1830s, white working-class women were learning this lesson as well. When New England mill owners lowered their wages in 1834, women workers did not meekly accept their fate. Nor did they ask for charity. They did agree that if there were "any in want, the Ladies will be compassionate and assist them." As for the mill hands themselves, they preferred "to have the disposing of our charities in our own hands; and as we are free, we would remain in possession of what kind Providence has bestowed upon us, and remain daughters of freemen still." Mill workers were well aware that charity was not free.

Rather than receive handouts, mill workers decided to walk out, leaving the mills short-staffed, to pressure owners into maintaining the wage rates. The probusiness *Boston Evening Transcript* reported that in Lowell, 800 strikers had formed a procession "and marched about town. We are told that one of the leaders mounted a pump and made a flaming . . . speech on the rights of women and the iniquities of the 'moneyed aristocracy,' which produced a powerful effect on her auditors, and they determined to 'have their own way if they died for it.'"

Mill workers had struck sporadically since 1824. Only after the 1834 turnouts, however, did women begin to develop local organizations to sustain their protests. Textile workers in Lowell formed the Factory Girls' Association in 1836 and immediately signed up over 2,500 members. Workers in other factory towns across New England followed Lowell's lead, developing local organizations to bring about strikes.

The hopes of the workers were dashed with the onset of the 1837 depression. With business down and labor plentiful, workers had little choice but to accept cuts in pay. But when the 1840s brought an upturn in both the national economy and the textile industry, a new generation of mill workers was ready to press their case again. Their activities would once again expand the things that women could do—the idea of "woman's sphere."

Women textile workers at first had difficulty coordinating their

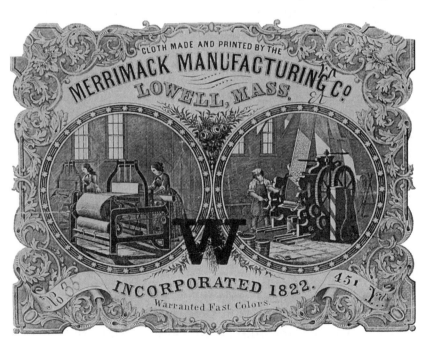

A cloth label from the Merrimack Manufacturing Co. in Lowell, Massachusetts, illustrates women workers weaving and printing calico.

actions with their male counterparts. Often, male workers did not see women's struggles as their own. During the 1840s, however, women workers joined forces with men through the movement to limit the work day to 10 hours, 6 days a week. Together, these women and men fought to raise wage rates and improve working conditions. Numerous mill workers came to hold important posts in both women's and mixed (male and female) organizations. Perhaps the most famous of these was Sarah Bagley, who seemed to be involved in every New England labor struggle during the mid-1840s.

Bagley was born in the early 1800s in Meredith, New Hampshire. She came to the Lowell mills just before the 1837 depression, and for seven years apparently worked without complaint. In 1844, when mill workers began organizing against longer working hours and increases in the pace of work, Bagley bloomed into a labor leader. She began by building up the newly formed Lowell Female Reform Association, an auxiliary of the New England Workingman's Association (NEWA). After increasing local membership from 5 to more than 800, she organized chapters in Manchester, Waltham, Nashua, Fall River, and other New England mill towns. During this time, she wrote for numerous reform papers, and for a time she edited the NEWA's paper, *Voice of Industry*.

In 1845, Bagley helped organize a petition drive to the Massachusetts legislature requesting a 10-hour-day law. The legislature, which was overwhelmingly probusiness, was finally compelled to form an investigative committee—the first ever to consider a labor dispute—after being besieged with thousands of signatures. The legislators figured they had found a way out, however. Of the eight mill workers they summoned as witnesses, six were women. Believing that no woman would dare to face an austere body like the Massachusetts legislature, the committee warned, "as the greater part of the petitioners are females, it will be necessary for them to make the defence, or we shall be under the necessity of laying the petition aside."

Sarah Bagley and her coworkers neither shirked their duty nor buckled under to the legislators' tough questioning. Among Bagley's colleagues that day were women who would become the stars of the women's labor movement—Huldah Stone and Eliza Hemingway among them. Despite their powerful testimony, the legislature, led

To the Senate and House of Representatives of the State of Massachusetts:

We, the undersigned, Operatives and Laborers of Lowell, in view of the alarming effects of the present number of hours which the Operatives in our Mills are required to labor, upon their health and happiness; and believing this system of tedious and protracted toil to exist, in a great degree, by virtue of legislative enactments, in opposition to the great principles of justice, equality and republicanism, laid down in the Declaration of Rights, so essential to the moral, mental and physical well-being of society, and the existence of a free and virtuous people; therefore, in justice to ourselves, to our fellow workers, and to posterity, we anxiously and hopefully invoke your aid and assistance in removing this oppressive burden, by enacting such a law, as will prohibit all incorporated companies from employing one set of hands more than ten hours per day.

That the present hours of labor are too long, and tend to aggrandize the capitalist and depress the laborer, is admitted by the good, the wise and philanthropic of the world; and we trust by every consideration of duty to your highly revered State, and the prosperity of her industrious population, and as just and righteous legislators, you will be induced to grant this reasonable petition; thereby saving our country from many of the calamities which have visited all people who suffer wealth and monopoly to feed upon the natural rights of the working classes.

Your petitioners would also call your attention to an article in the Factory Regulations, which is the cause of much injustice and oppression on the part of the corporations, and which reads as follows:

"All persons entering into the employment of the Company are considered as engaged for twelve months, and those who leave sooner, or do not comply with these regulations, will not be entitled to a regular discharge."

The effects of this regulation are becoming every day more grievous, giving to the manufacturer great power over the operative, and leading to monopoly and wrong. Your memorialists firmly believe that this combination is entered into to destroy the independence of the operatives, and place their labor within the control of the manufacturers—an illustration of which we briefly subjoin :— Mary A—— engages to work for the M—— Company, in the city of Lowell; according to the regulation she is considered engaged for one year; but for some good reason, perhaps ill treatment from her overseer, she wishes to leave, and applies for a "a regular discharge"—it is refused, and her name is immediately sent to all the other Corporations, as being upon the "black list;" and should she apply for work she is denied, no matter how destitute her condition. Thus we consider a "people's Legislature" in duty bound to interfere for the protection of the weak and defenceless against the combined strength of capital and organized power.

John Simpson   Sarah G. Bagley
John Santon   Miguel Daniel
John W. Davis   Our Tree hist Mark
J. C. Ferres   Twelve Mien
Geo W. Evans   Eugene Tummuthy
Wm Sweetser   Chain M prest
John Smith   Teicommal Leonard
Daniel K Downing Patrick Parlin
Shepard Watson   Samuel Zickerman
Lorenzo Kinney   Kerbel French
B Hayden   Paine Slare
Wm N Crosby   Daniel C Plummer
Wm Gale   John Obrien
O York   Davie Austin
Alvin B Gales   Alason Mitchel
Thomas Moor   Andrew McKnight
J Monroe Shebby   Robert Polen
George Daly   William Orr

TIME TABLE OF THE LOWELL MILLS,

Arranged to make the working time throughout the year average 11 hours per day.

TO TAKE EFFECT SEPTEMBER 21st., 1853.

The Standard time being that of the meridian of Lowell, as shown by the Regulator Clock of AMOS SANBORN, Post Office Corner, Central Street.

From March 20th to September 19th, inclusive.

COMMENCE WORK, at 6.30 A. M. LEAVE OFF WORK, at 6.30 P. M., except on Saturday Evenings.
BREAKFAST at 6 A. M. DINNER, at 12 M. Commence Work, after dinner, 12.45 P. M.

From September 20th to March 19th, inclusive.

COMMENCE WORK at 7.00 A. M. LEAVE OFF WORK, at 7.00 P. M., except on Saturday Evenings.
BREAKFAST at 6.30 A. M. DINNER, at 12.30 P.M. Commence Work, after dinner, 1.15 P. M.

BELLS.

From March 20th to September 19th, inclusive.

Morning Bells.	*Dinner Bells.*	*Evening Bells.*
First bell,..........4.30 A. M.	Ring out,...............12.00 M.	Ring out,............6.30 P. M.
Second, 5.30 A. M.; Third, 6.20.	Ring in,............12.35 P. M.	Except on Saturday Evenings.

From September 20th to March 19th, inclusive.

Morning Bells.	*Dinner Bells.*	*Evening Bells.*
First bell,..........5.00 A. M.	Ring out,...............12.30 P. M.	Ring out at............7.00 P. M.
Second, 6.00 A. M.; Third, 6.50.	Ring in,............1.05 P. M.	Except on Saturday Evenings.

SATURDAY EVENING BELLS.

During APRIL, MAY, JUNE, JULY, and AUGUST, Ring Out, at 6.00 P. M.
The remaining Saturday Evenings in the year, ring out as follows :

SEPTEMBER.	NOVEMBER.	JANUARY.
First Saturday, ring out 6.00 P. M.	Third Saturday ring out 4.00 P. M.	Third Saturday ring out 4.25 P. M.
Second " " 5.45 "	Fourth " " 3.55 "	Fourth " " 4.35 "
Third " " 5.30 "		
Fourth " " 5.20 "	DECEMBER.	FEBRUARY.
	First Saturday, ring out 3.50 P. M.	First Saturday, ring out 4.45 P. M.
OCTOBER.	Second " " 3.55 "	Second " " 4.55 "
First Saturday, ring out 5.05 P. M.	Third " " 3.55 "	Third " " 5.00 "
Second " " 4.55 "	Fourth " " 4.00 "	Fourth " " 5.10 "
Third " " 4.45 "	Fifth " " 4.00 "	
Fourth " " 4.35 "		MARCH.
Fifth " " 4.25 "	JANUARY.	First Saturday, ring out 5.25 P. M.
	First Saturday, ring out 4.10 P. M.	Second " " 5.30 "
NOVEMBER.	Second " " 4.15 "	Third " " 5.35 "
First Saturday, ring out 4.15 P. M.		Fourth " " 5.45 "
Second "· " 4.05 "		

YARD GATES will be opened at the first stroke of the bells for entering or leaving the Mills.

•.• *SPEED GATES commence hoisting three minutes before commencing work.*

The timetable from the Lowell mills was set up so that workers labored for an average of 11 hours per day. The working hours were announced by a rigid bell schedule.

by probusiness editor William Schouler, offered no criticism of the industry in its final report. The women workers had the last word, however. After promising to "consign William Schouler to the obscurity he so justly deserves," they organized to defeat him in his bid for reelection as Lowell's state senator.

The labor struggles of the 1840s also broadened women's perspective about who they were and what was possible. Just as evangelical reformers had developed an understanding of women as a group, so too did the textile workers. The workers, however, began to see themselves as members of both a *gender* (that is, their sex) and a *class* (their position in society). One woman, writing in the

Opposite: *This old, faded petition from Lowell mill workers to the Massachusetts legislature asks for a law limiting the workday to 10 hours.*

labor paper *Zion's Herald,* proudly proclaimed, "I am heartily glad when anything is done to elevate that class to which it is my lot to belong. We are a band of sisters and must have sympathy for each other's woes."

Middle-class critics complained bitterly about the public activities of textile workers. Claiming that moral reform was an extension of motherhood was one thing, critics argued. But what possible justification could "these Amazons" have for so brazenly violating the niceties of domesticity? The strikers, however, seemed to have cared little for these middle-class notions. Instead, they looked to the ideals of the American Revolution. To the strikers, their actions were the natural course for "daughters of freemen" to take.

Some workers used their strike experience to challenge the ideal of domesticity itself. One woman, writing in a prolabor paper in 1845, declared:

> Woman is never thought to be out of her *sphere* at home; in the nursery, in the kitchen, over a hot stove cooking from morning till evening—over a washtub, or toiling in a cotton factory 14 hours per day. But let her once step out, plead the cause of right and humanity, plead the wrongs of her slave sister of the South or of the [worker] of the North, . . . and a cry is raised against her, "*out of her sphere.*"

Women workers were beginning to make connections: between their oppression as women and as workers; between their own oppression and that of African-American slaves. Huldah Stone saw the vast possibilities of this new way of seeing when she declared that the textile workers

> do not regard [the 10-hour movement] as an end, but only as one step toward the end to be attained. They deeply feel that their work will never be accomplished until slavery and oppression, mental, physical, and religious, shall have been done away with and Christianity in it original simplicity and pristine beauty shall be re-established and practiced.

Who would have foreseen that Isabella Marshall Graham's first careful steps would have been overtaken by Huldah Stone's bold strides into the public arena? Who might have suspected that the orderly mills and boardinghouses would have produced "Amazons" who challenged the basis of the American social and economic system? Such upheavals, however, were the harbingers of things to come.

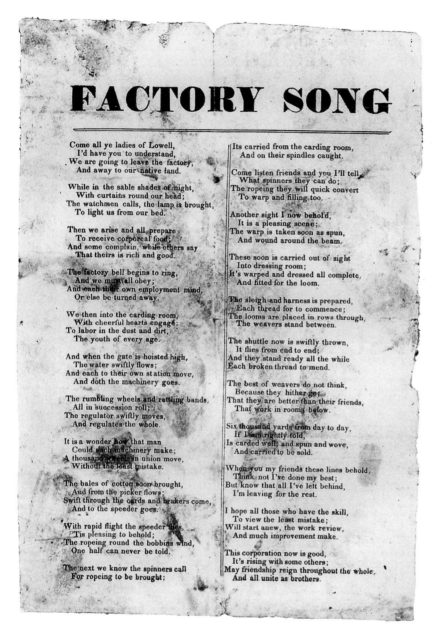

This factory song was probably written by a mill worker for contribution to a company newspaper.

The textile industry would soon undergo sweeping changes that would transform the workers' movement. And the era's greatest struggle against oppression—the antislavery movement—had only just begun.

EIGHTH

ANNUAL REPORT

OF THE

BOSTON FEMALE

ANTI-SLAVERY SOCIETY.

PRESENTED OCTOBER 13, 1841.

Boston:

PUBLISHED BY THE SOCIETY,

25 CORNHILL.

1841.

CHAPTER 7

THE POLITICS OF RESISTANCE: WOMEN AGAINST SLAVERY

I t was 1835 and they knew there would be trouble. Boston's Mayor Theodore Lyman had begged Maria Weston Chapman, the leader of the Boston Female Antislavery Society, to cancel the interracial antislavery meeting that night. He knew that the mere presence of the radical abolitionist William Lloyd Garrison would be sure to stir up an angry mob. And the presence of white and black women together—well, that was just tossing kerosene on the fire. And fire there very well might be—abolitionists had been burned in effigy before, and there was a good chance that someone would next take a torch to the meeting hall.

Chapman held her ground, however, insisting that principle had to stand fast in the face of cowardly intimidation. Once in the hall that night, as a howling mob outside shouted obscenities and threatened worse, Chapman was even more resolute. Responding to Lyman's last-ditch appeal to cancel the meeting, Chapman replied, "If this is the last bulwark of freedom, we might as well die here." After Garrison spoke briefly, he was hustled out the back door. The mob caught on to the ruse, however, and proceeded to drag Garrison through town at the end of a rope. Back at the meeting hall, Chapman calmly ordered the women to group themselves in pairs, one black and one white. The women then passed through the mob, "their

The Boston Female Anti-Slavery Society accepted both blacks and whites as members, a policy that many white Bostonians bitterly and sometimes violently objected to.

An 1847 daguerreotype of Maria Weston Chapman, the leader of the Boston Female Antislavery Society.

hands folded in their cotton gloves, their eyes busily identifying the genteel leaders of the mob."

While abolitionist women were daring the wrath of northern mobs to vanquish "the awful sin of slavery," southern slave women were resisting slavery on a more personal level. Many years after regaining her freedom, Eliza Washington recalled how she had first stood up to her mistress. After her mistress scolded Washington for scrubbing the floor improperly, Washington "sassed her, and she struck me with her hand." That slap set off a chain of events that Washington savored many years later in the retelling: "Thinks I, it's a good time now to dress you out, and damned if I won't do it. I set down my tools and squared for a fight. The first whack, I struck her a hell of a blow with my fist. I didn't knock her entirely through the panels of the door, but her landing against the door made a terrible smash, and I hurt her so badly that all were frightened out of their wits and I didn't know myself but what I'd killed the old devil." Although Eliza received a whipping, her mistress refrained from slapping her after that.

Both northern abolitionist women and southern slave women put themselves at risk in opposing slavery. Though abolitionists did not always have to face angry mobs, they did continually experience both the subtle and not-so-subtle forms of harassment that befall those who champion unpopular causes. In return, they hoped to destroy the institution of slavery and return some measure of dignity to the lives of African Americans. The focus of slave women's energies was more immediate, and the threat of violent reprisal more likely. Slave women knew quite clearly that slavery was unjust, but they were more concerned with the day-to-day struggle to survive. They constantly had to measure their attempts at resistance against the probability of physical and emotional damage their masters and mistresses might inflict on them. Both abolitionists and slaves were working to oppose the system of slavery, but they had very different concerns—and they chose very different means.

Slave women's acts of resistance often differed from men's. Although women had taken an active part in slave rebellions in the past, by the mid-1700s these uprisings were largely all-male activities. Slave men came to view uprisings as a chance to reassert the warrior role that their forefathers had taken in Africa. After 1750, because slaveholders passed numerous laws to hinder slave organization, rebellions also became less frequent. Instead, slaves chose to resist on a more individual level.

Some slaves took pride in their work and were fortunate to have a master and mistress who actually lived by the Christian precepts laid out in slaveholding literature. Even in these homes, however, a slave might resist the basic inhumanity of a slave's existence. One

A page from an antislavery tract illustrating the brutal punishment of a slave. Although they risked physical punishment, slave women sometimes resisted their mistress or master in subtle ways, by avoiding a chore or serving spoiled food, for example.

Single male slaves were more likely than an entire family to run away. Women usually had several children to care for and had no opportunity to leave the plantation, whereas skilled male slaves were allowed to travel on the roads.

possibility was fleeing the plantation for freedom in the North. Once northern states began abolishing slavery after the American Revolution, slave men increasingly chose this as an option. Fewer slave women took this course, largely because they were unwilling to abandon their children. Also, those slave men trained as carpenters, blacksmiths, and at other skilled jobs were often sent out to earn money for the master. They had more opportunity to escape and were a more common sight on southern roads. A woman alone was more likely to attract unwelcome attention.

Some slave women did escape, and a few became celebrities. Ellen Craft, one of the most famous runaways of the time, convinced her husband, William, to join her in an elaborate ruse to gain their freedom. While Craft's owners were as kindly as slave owners could be, she feared that if she had any children they would be sold away from her. Craft, who was light-skinned, arranged to be dressed as a man, complete with a top hat. She obscured her face with a handkerchief, meant to simulate treatment for a toothache, and bound her arm in a sling, so that it would not be discovered that she could not write. Her husband came along posing as "Mr. Johnson's" servant. When William balked at this scheme, she implored, "Come, William, don't be a coward! Get me the clothes and I promise you we shall be free in a few days." And after securing passage on a northbound steamer, they were. Both became active in the abolitionist crusade.

Other women concocted imaginative deceptions to gain their

Lear Green devised a scheme in which she shipped herself from Baltimore to Philadelphia in a sailor's chest, but most women found escaping from slavery an unlikely option.

freedom. Lear Green, a house servant in Baltimore, escaped by packing herself in a large sailor's chest and then having it shipped to Philadelphia. Such tales were quickly publicized in northern papers eager to demonstrate cracks in the southern slave system. Perhaps the most famous runaway, Harriet Tubman, escaped from her Maryland plantation in 1849 after the rest of her family chose to remain in the South. Over the next 10 years she led expeditions to free hundreds of slaves, including many members of the family she had left behind. Her exploits would gain her much renown among northern abolitionists and much hatred among slaveholders.

But, without running away, it was still possible to resist the daily indignities and physical hardships of slavery. Sometimes slave women attempted dire retribution against their tormentors. Although whites were forbidden to sell chemicals to slaves, slave women knew about the deadly effects of numerous plants. A particularly evil master or mistress might find out too late that a sampling of a poisonous plant had been added to the soup. Other slave owners might find ground-up glass in their drinks. In most cases, however, a perpetrator was either discovered or invented, and some slave paid the price with his or her life.

Some slave women retaliated against their owners when they perceived themselves to be punished beyond what they considered to be just. Ellen Cragin recalled how her mother had reacted when her master's teenage son began to whip her for falling asleep while working the loom: "She took a pole out of the loom and beat him nearly to death." When he begged her to stop, she replied, "I'm going to kill you. These black titties suckled you, and then you come out here to beat me." Cragin noted that when her mother finally stopped, "he wasn't able to walk."

When slave women were unable to take such actions against their owners, they sometimes directed drastic measures against themselves. One woman, upon learning that she was to be sold and separated from her children, chopped off her fingers with a cleaver and ruined the sale. Other women refused to see any more of their babies sold off to distant plantations. After one mother was forced to give up three young children within several years, she took her fourth-born, and according to one observer, "gave it something out of the bottle and pretty soon it was dead." Since both infanticide and induced abortions were viewed by slaveholding society as a crime against the master's property, mothers found guilty of these crimes were usually sentenced to death.

Not all resistance took on such tragic proportions. Often women would simply make work in the field and the Big House go less smoothly than it might have. The trick was to make their actions appear as accidental as possible, so that the milk would seem to sour mysteriously. However, since slaves were usually whipped for even the appearance of wrongdoing, a punishment was often forthcoming. Given the enormous risks a slave took in resisting, it is not surprising that many chose simply to get along with the system as best they could. As one slave woman put it, "If your head is in the lion's mouth, it's best to pet him a little."

African-American women who lived in the North realized that their freedom enabled them to fight slavery in ways that their southern sisters did not have. While northern blacks suffered enormous prejudice and occasionally violence, they also enjoyed certain basic rights and protections not accorded to slaves. The first Female Antislavery Society was organized in Salem, Massachusetts, in 1832. An outgrowth of the Colored Female Religious and Moral Society of Salem, the Female Antislavery Society pledged in its constitution to work both against slavery and for the improvement of blacks. Its combination of self-help with abolitionist activities would be replicated in other black women's antislavery organizations.

Some black abolitionists, such as Maria Stewart of Boston, at-

Old South Leaflets.

No. 78.

The Liberator.

Vol. I.   No. 1.

WILLIAM LLOYD GARRISON and
ISAAC KNAPP, *Publishers.*

BOSTON, MASSACHUSETTS.— Saturday, January 1, 1831.

Our Country is the World — Our Countrymen are Mankind.

THE SALUTATION.

To date my being from the opening year,
I come, a stranger in this busy sphere,
Where some I meet perchance may pause and ask,
What is my name, my purpose, or my task?

My name is 'LIBERATOR'!   I propose
To hurl my shafts at freedom's deadliest foes!
My task is hard — for I am charged to save
Man from his brother! — to redeem the slave!

Ye who may hear, and yet condemn my cause,
Say, shall the best of Nature's holy laws
Be trodden down? and shall her open veins
Flow but for cement to her offspring's chains?

Art thou a parent? shall thy children be
Rent from thy breast, like branches from the tree,
And doom'd to servitude, in helplessness,
On other shores, and thou ask no redress?

Thou, in whose bosom glows the sacred flame
Of filial love, say, if the tyrant came,
To force thy parent shrieking from thy sight,
Would thy heart bleed — *because thy face is white?*

Art thou a brother? shall thy sister twine
Her feeble arm in agony on thine,
And thou not lift the heel, nor aim the blow
At him who bears her off to life-long wo?

THE LIBERATOR is published weekly at No. 6 Merchants' Hall. WM. L. GARRISON, *Editor.*
STEPHEN FOSTER, *Printer.*   Terms, two dollars per annum, payable in advance.

The first page of the January 1831 issue of William Lloyd Garrison's The Liberator. *This newspaper became a standard-bearer for radical abolitionists and eventually supported women's abolitionist activities.*

tempted to fight slavery not by appealing to whites, but by imploring blacks to work towards self-improvement. Stewart began her campaign in 1832 after reading an editorial in Garrison's newspaper, the *Liberator,* extolling the special power of women's moral influence. Deeply religious, Stewart submitted several essays to the

Liberator on morality, Christian duty, and African-American conditions. Garrison published these essays in his paper and then issued them as pamphlets. After he encouraged Stewart to present her ideas to black audiences, she began her speaking career.

Stewart believed that because whites ignored the conditions of blacks—both free and slave—blacks should "turn [their] attention to knowledge and improvement." Once blacks elevated themselves, "even those who now point at us with fingers of scorn will aid and befriend us. It is no use to sit with hands folded, lamenting our wretched condition; if no one will promote or respect us, let us promote and respect ourselves." Stewart was particularly concerned about earning respect for black women, urging them "to strive by their examples, both in public and private, to assist those who are endeavoring to stop the strong current of prejudice."

Despite Stewart's call for black women's prominence in the abolitionist movement—because of it, in fact—she was often harassed or criticized for her speeches. Most African-American men were no more ready to accept women as public speakers than white men were. In 1833, Stewart gave her farewell address, in which she acknowledged that the black community was not yet ready for a forceful woman speaker. She asked her audience, "What if I am a woman? Did not God raise up Deborah to be a mother and a judge in Israel? Did not Queen Esther save the lives of the Jews? If such women once existed, be no longer astonished, then, that God at this eventful period should raise up your females to strive." It was a question other abolitionists, both black and white, would be presenting to their male counterparts.

While some black women abolitionists preferred to work in groups separate from whites, others chose to join integrated organizations. Interracial groups such as the Boston Female Antislavery Association directly challenged northern assumptions about the need to separate the races, as the incident of the Boston mob demonstrates. The Philadelphia Antislavery Association, which had almost as many black as white charter members in 1833, attracted fierce criticism and occasional reprisals for its effrontery. In 1838, in a repetition of the Boston mob scene, an abolitionist group was surrounded at the newly built Pennsylvania Hall. After tossing stones in the window, blocking the doors, and threatening the attendees as they departed, the

The inscription on this bronze antislavery medal from 1838 is a version of a quotation from former slave Sojourner Truth, who declared: "A'n't I a woman and a sister?"

Orator Wendell Phillips speaks at an antislavery meeting on the Boston Common. There were a few black citizens in the crowd, but many abolition groups were not racially integrated.

mob—unhindered by any police presence—burned the building to the ground. A spokesman for the mob explained that the hall had been destroyed because the "audience [was] promiscuously mixed up of blacks and whites."

Such attacks caused some conservative abolitionists to suggest that black and white women remain apart while fighting slavery. Lucretia Mott, the leading white woman abolitionist in Philadelphia, criticized these "psuedo-abolitionists," who "left no means untried to expunge from our minutes a resolution to social intercourse with our colored brethren." When the Philadelphia mayor asked Mott that white women "avoid unnecessary walking with colored people," she replied, "We have never made a parade of walking with colored people and should do as we've done before—walk with them as occasion offered."

The Philadelphia society was able to maintain its vigorous integrationist stance, thanks in part to whites like Mott and her sister, Martha Coffin Wright. They favored an egalitarian stand, the belief that men and women, blacks and whites should participate equally in the fight against slavery. But these efforts would have been for naught if not for the presence of strong black women abolitionists like Charlotte Forten and her remarkable daughters, Margaretta, Harriet, and Sarah Louise. (Charlotte Forten's namesake and granddaughter, Charlotte Forten Grimké, became well known as an educator.) Charlotte Forten was a founding member of the Philadelphia Female Antislavery Society, and Margaretta served in numerous official capacities; Harriet was active in the Underground Railroad during the 1850s with her husband, Robert Purvis; and Sarah Louise frequently contributed to the *Liberator* and the *Abolitionist*. With these activities, the family worked to strengthen ties between black and white abolitionists in Philadelphia and across the country.

Not all local antislavery societies were as open to black members as the Philadelphia group. The Boston, Rochester, Salem, and Lynn (Massachusetts) societies were integrated, but the New York City society split over whether to accept black women as members. Several midwestern cities, which established antislavery societies, also wrangled over the relations of black and white members. But integrationists, who believed in both races working together, were prominent enough in the national society to support the candidacies of such leading black abolitionists as Susan Paul, Martha Ball, and Grace Douglass to important positions in the national organization.

A number of white abolitionists suffered persecution for their integrationist or antislavery beliefs. Lydia Maria Child's successful literary career came to a crashing halt when she began to espouse both antislavery and integrationist sentiments. Although her husband had been an abolitionist for several years, Child did not embrace the cause until she met Garrison in 1831. Child later recalled that Garrison "got hold of the strings of my conscience and pulled me into reforms." Two years later, she published *An Appeal in Favor of that Class of Americans Called Africans*.

One of the first antislavery books published in America, the *Appeal* galvanized numerous important reformers to the abolitionists' cause, including Wendell Phillips, a Boston aristocrat, and Charles Sumner, a U.S. senator from Massachusetts. The effect on Child's place in Boston's literary and genteel society was far less pleasant. Her past associates were particularly upset at her denunciation of laws against mixed marriages and her support for integrating churches, theaters, and stagecoaches. She was barred from many lecture halls, and her reading public rejected her next works on domestic subjects.

The uproar caught Child by surprise. She later recalled that after the *Appeal* was published, "old dreams vanished, old associates

The literary career of Lydia Maria Child changed course after she was ostracized by genteel Boston society for supporting racial integration. Child turned from writing novels to focusing on antislavery writing and editing projects.

departed, and all things became new." For Child, making a living at writing was a necessity as well as a vocation, since her husband rarely earned enough to support them. She plunged headlong into a number of abolitionist writing and editing projects, for a time editing the *National Anti-Slavery Standard*. Although she had some commercial successes (including her *Letters from New York,* in 1843 and 1845), she was never again the darling of middle- and upper-class literary society. Sarah Josepha Hale, surveying Child's abolitionist writings, lamented, "Her fine genius, her soul's wealth has been wasted." Child herself had no such regrets.

Unlike Child, Prudence Crandall did not embrace the abolitionist cause through a spiritual conversion. Rather, fate helped transform a rather staid, respectable New England life into a quest for reform. Crandall had been hired by the leading citizens of Canterbury, Connecticut, to run the Canterbury Female Boarding School. All went well for several years until Sarah Harris, a young black girl, asked to be admitted to the school. Harris told Crandall, "I want to get a little more learning, enough if possible to teach colored children, and if you will admit me to your school, I shall forever be under the greatest obligation to you. If you think that it will be the means of injuring you, I will not insist on the favor."

Up to that point, Crandall had not taken an active part in the abolitionist cause. Having attended a Quaker boarding school, however, she was predisposed against slavery. She was given further encouragement by her maid, an African-American woman who was about to marry the local distributor of the *Liberator*. Crandall, realizing that she might face some complaints from Canterbury students and their parents, nevertheless decided to accept Harris as a pupil. In time, she hoped, those who protested the girl's presence would come to accept her. Instead, parents removed their children from the school one by one, and the school's more traditional supporters demanded that Harris be expelled. Crandall chose to close the school instead.

Crandall, however, had just begun to fight. After gathering advise and support from abolitionists throughout the Northeast, Crandall returned to Canterbury to establish a school for "Young Ladies and Little Misses of Color." Twenty young women from surrounding areas and as far away as Boston and New York City attended the

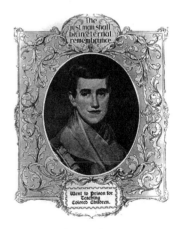

Prudence Crandall embraced the abolitionist cause after the town of Canterbury, Connecticut, was outraged when she admitted a black student to her school for girls.

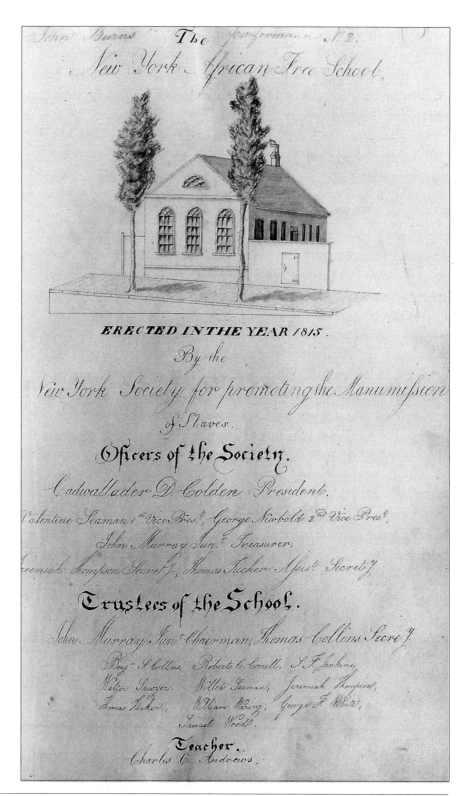

Because blacks were usually barred from public school, privately supported schools in the North for free blacks, such as the New York African School, provided one of the few ways for them to receive an education.

school. In response, the town of Canterbury virtually declared war on Crandall and her students.

Town leaders first threatened to arrest her students as vagrants. Connecticut legislators then passed a law making it illegal to educate a black pupil from another state. Eventually, an appeals court threw the case out, perhaps realizing that it raised some knotty constitutional issues. Before her victory, however, she went to jail three separate times for defying the law. Canterburians tried more direct methods as well. They smashed the school's windows, tossed stones and rotten eggs at students and teachers, and spoiled the school's well with manure. No merchant in town would sell supplies to the school, and doctors refused to visit.

Crandall, aided by abolitionists from neighboring communities and her resolute students, refused to yield. As if in a fort under siege, they had to cart in food and water through a gauntlet of taunting townsfolk. The problems of the school became a rallying cry for abolitionists, and contributions were sent from across the North. Eventually, however, the siege became a frontal assault. One night, a mob set fire to the basement. After smashing some battering rams against the doors and walls, they trashed the classrooms while Crandall and her terrified students huddled upstairs. The next day, Crandall surrendered, unwilling to put her students' lives at risk. After closing the school, she moved with her husband to Illinois, where she continued to be active in abolitionist and women's rights causes.

Prudence Crandall's and Maria Lydia Child's experiences demonstrate the depth of racism that existed in the North. Even many Northerners who were opposed to southern slavery still had little use for the idea of black equality, and even less use for any attempt at racial integration. Soon after Garrison launched the *Liberator* in 1829, a split appeared in the antislavery ranks between those promoting black equality and those merely wishing to phase out slavery. At the same time, the issue of women's place within the movement also became a central point of contention between the two camps.

In 1833, speaking at a convention in Philadelphia, Garrison called for the founding of a national antislavery association. Despite the presence of numerous influential abolitionist women in the city, women were barred from joining the newly formed American Antislavery

William Lloyd Garrison called for the creation of a national antislavery society in 1833. Women were at first barred from the organization, even though they had been important crusaders against slavery.

Society. Apparently, while Garrison had embraced the ideal of immediate emancipation and black equality, he had not yet equated these goals with women's rights. The women who had witnessed the proceedings had other ideas. Led by Lucretia Mott and Charlotte Forten, they immediately formed the Philadelphia Female Anti-Slavery Society.

The first speakers to bring the intertwined issues of abolition and women's rights to a national audience were raised in the heart of slaveholding society. Angelina and Sarah Grimké were born to a prominent South Carolina plantation family. Both had some misgivings about the treatment of slaves when they were growing up, and they recorded in their diaries their conflicts between their sense of Christian morality and the reality of southern slave society. During a visit to Philadelphia in 1819, Sarah became attracted to the Quakers' professions of simplicity and piety. Two years later, she moved to Philadelphia. Ten years after that, Angelina followed her sister north, unable to reconcile her personal beliefs with the horrors of the slave system that surrounded her.

Despite their abandonment of the South, the sisters did not become active abolitionists until Angelina joined the Philadelphia Female Antislavery Society in 1835. A year later, she published *An Appeal to the Christian Women of the South,* which instantly drew the public's attention. The Grimké family was well established in South Carolina, and a firsthand account of slavery's sinfulness from such a privileged person sent shock waves through both North and South. The pamphlet was particularly radical in that it urged southern women to lead the way in the fight against slavery. Postal workers often confiscated and then burned copies once they entered the South. Meanwhile, South Carolina politicians tried to outdo each other in denouncing the woman they saw as a traitor to her people.

In 1836, both sisters attended a lecture by Theodore Weld, a leading abolitionist orator. Weld's talk inspired Sarah to publish *Epistle to the Clergy of the Southern States,* which argued that the Bible did not condone slavery, as many southern ministers had insisted. The Grimkés did not neglect the North, however. Two years later, Angelina wrote *Appeal to the Women of the Nominally Free States,* an attack on northern racism and the complicity of northern racists in prolonging slavery.

Angelina (top) and Sarah Grimké were raised on a South Carolina plantation but moved to Philadelphia as adults. The sisters became leading abolitionists and advocates for women's rights, often linking the two causes in their fiery lectures and writings.

At this time both sisters were speaking to groups of women who flocked to hear their firsthand accounts of life in slave society. Angelina was particularly active, often speaking six nights in a row. Her unique perspective began to attract men to the audience, despite early efforts to restrict attendance to women. In 1838, she became the first woman to address the Massachusetts legislature on behalf of the hundreds of women's antislavery petitions that were pouring in.

All this notoriety was bound to gain the attention of the more conservative members of society. In 1837, the Congregational ministers of Massachusetts issued a strong condemnation of the Grimkés' behavior. "We invite your attention to the dangers which at present seem to threaten the female character with widespread and permanent injury," it warned. "We appreciate the [humbleness] of women in advancing the cause of religion at home and abroad in Sabbath schools and in all such associations associated with the modesty of her sex. But when she yields the power that was given her for her protection, then her character becomes unnatural." The ministers were particularly upset that the Grimkés had pursued these unnatural activities in "promiscuous audiences" of women and men.

Upon reading of the pastoral letter, Angelina Grimké wrote Weld, "We are placed very unexpectedly in a very trying situation, in the forefront of an entirely new contest—a contest for the *rights of woman* as a moral, intelligent and responsible being." Many male abolitionists believed, however, that this was a contest not worth fighting. Weld responded that women's rights was "an extraneous issue. . . . We cannot push Abolition forward," he urged Angelina, "until we take up the stumbling block out of the road."

Encouraged by Garrison's conversion to their position, the Grimkés argued that women's rights were not an obstacle, but part of the foundation of abolitionism and social justice in general. Sarah Grimké produced *Letters on the Equality of the Sexes and the Condition of Women* in 1838, and Angelina contributed a series on the subject to the *Liberator*. Proving their continued popularity, they sold out a series of six lectures at Boston's Odeon Hall in the spring of 1838.

The Grimkés' remarkable speaking career came to an end several months later. It was Angelina who delivered the impassioned lecture the fateful night that the mob burned Pennsylvania Hall. Exhausted by the demands and dangers of her speaking engagements,

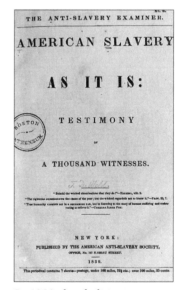

In 1839 the abolitionists Theodore Weld and the Grimké sisters published these extracts from southern newspapers describing the evils of slavery.

she suffered a mental collapse shortly thereafter. Having married Theodore Weld days before the burning of Philadelphia Hall, Angelina retired with her husband and her sister to recuperate. Although the sisters produced some abolitionist tracts in the next few years, they effectively withdrew from the public movement.

Other women abolitionists followed the Grimkés into the breach they had created for the "woman question." Among the most prominent was Abigail Kelley Foster, who helped found the Lynn Antislavery Society in 1835. She became one of the early pioneers who insisted on women's right to speak publicly about politics. Refuting those who would consign her to "woman's sphere," she proclaimed in the *Connecticut Observer*, in 1840, "Whatever ways and means are right for men to adopt in reforming the world, are right also for women to adopt in pursuing the same subject." She was such a powerful speaker that she inevitably raised significant sums for the abolitionist cause whenever she lectured. Along with Lucretia Mott, she served as an inspiration and example to a whole generation of abolitionists and women's rights advocates, including Paulina Wright Davis, Lucy Stone, and Susan B. Anthony.

Although the "woman question" was not the only issue splitting radicals and conservatives in the antislavery movement, it became the wedge that forced a split. The supporters of women abolitionists came out on top, but the minority issued a bitter denunciation of the outcome that suggested the fight was not yet over. In 1840, those opposing women's influence in the society—a group that included many powerful men—formed a separate society. This all-male society would lead the way in pressing the cause of antislavery in the political arena. Meanwhile, the American Antislavery Society quickly placed Lydia Maria Child, Maria Weston Chapman, and Lucretia Mott on its executive committee, and it continued its efforts to convince the American people of the morality of women's participation in public debate and the immorality of slavery.

Before the final breakup, there was still one more battle to be fought between the two sides. In the summer of 1840, the American Antislavery Society attempted to have Lucretia Mott serve as one of its delegates at the World Antislavery Convention in London. The conservatives in the international delegations prevailed, and Mott was forced to watch the proceedings from the gallery.

This affront to Mott proved to have a more formidable impact on the history of women's rights than on the fight against slavery. For Elizabeth Cady Stanton, who attended the convention during her honeymoon with her husband, the abolitionist Henry Stanton, the convention provided a wholly unexpected enlightenment. Stanton, destined to be among the key leaders of the women's rights movement throughout the 19th century, was asked on her return what most impressed her about England. She replied immediately, "Lucretia Mott." She later reminisced, "I shall never forget the look of recognition she gave me when she saw by my remarks that I fully comprehended the problems of women's rights. Mrs. Mott was to me an entire new revelation of womanhood."

Following the convention, an unexpected—even unthinkable—notion came into their heads. Elizabeth Stanton later recalled, "As Lucretia Mott and Elizabeth Cady Stanton wended their way arm in arm down Great Queen Street that night, reviewing the exciting scenes of the day, they agreed to hold a woman's rights convention on their return to America, as the men to whom they had just listened had manifested their great need of some education on that question."

Eight years later, they achieved their goal.

At the World Antislavery Convention in London in 1840, Lucretia Mott was not allowed to serve as an American delegate because she was a woman. That disappointment inspired Mott and other women abolitionists to turn their attention to women's rights.

Equal Rights

VOL I, No. 18.
FIVE CENTS

OFFICIAL WEEKLY OF
THE NATIONAL WOMAN'S PARTY

SATURDAY, JUNE 16, 1923

Drawn by Nina E. Allender.

OUR BEST TRIBUTE IS TO FINISH THE WORK THEY BEGAN

CHAPTER 8

1848:
THE YEAR OF
REVOLUTION

Eighteen forty-eight was a momentous year for American women, as it was for men and women across the world. During the spring, revolutions against tyrannical governments were initiated in Germany, Italy, France, and the Austro-Hungarian empire. At first the revolutions appeared to succeed, and the besieged governments made numerous concessions in order to stave off complete collapse. Liberal constitutions promising more democratic participation and personal liberty were adopted, and various emperors and kings temporarily fled their capitals.

By autumn, however, the revolutions had collapsed, and the repressive governments reasserted themselves. Most of the liberal and radical revolutionaries were forced to flee Europe, and they were joined by those simply hoping to escape the chaos. American shipping companies also began regular transatlantic service between the United States and Europe in 1848. The United States, long considered by Europeans to be a place of boundless opportunities, became the destination of the majority of European refugees.

War was not the only reason for European immigration. A deadly cholera epidemic caused many to flee during 1847 and 1848. Crops in many of the European countries failed between 1845 and 1848. In Ireland, the potato crop was attacked by a blight that destroyed most

A 1923 issue of Equal Rights *magazine pays tribute to the women who started the American fight for women's rights at Seneca Falls in 1848.*

of the island's staple food. More than a million people died of starvation and disease, and a million and a half fled the country. Two out of every three of these immigrants landed in the United States.

Irish and Germans had been immigrating to the United States in small but significant numbers since the colonial era. This sudden surge, however, was something different. Between 1847 and 1857, more than 3 million immigrants entered the United States, with a third coming from Ireland and a third from Germany. As the Civil War began in 1860, European immigrants made up 15 percent of the white population.

The new immigration helped bring significant changes to American women. Immigrant women became a new source of cheap labor, largely replacing rural New England women as workers in the mills. Irish women were much more likely than Anglo-Protestant women to accept jobs as domestics, and thus answered the demand for house servants among the middle and upper classes. The new immigrants solidified the various ethnic neighborhoods that earlier Irish and German immigrants had established in urban areas, challenging the influence of the mainstream Anglo and Protestant culture. All of

Irish immigrants are packed onto this boat leaving for the United States. The surge in Irish immigration provided a new and cheap source of labor for New England mills and for white families eager to hire domestic servants.

these changes would have a significant impact as the United States transformed itself from an agricultural to an industrial nation in the second half of the 19th century.

The year 1848 also brought the Mexican-American War to a close, thus making "immigrants" of thousands of Hispanics who lived in the Southwest. With the signing of the Treaty of Guadalupe Hidalgo, Mexico was forced to cede to the United States all of the territory north of the Rio Grande and the Gila River and south of Oregon Country for a cash settlement. Hispanics would now have to live under the laws of the United States and would have to face the land hunger of the incoming Americans. They would soon find themselves losing political, cultural, and economic power in the land they had once controlled. American Indian tribes within the new territory would find themselves similarly beset by American settlers and the U.S. Army. The U.S. Army would soon wage a war of annihilation against those tribes not willing to submit to life on newly established reservations.

In California, these transformations were accelerated by the discovery of gold at Sutter's Mill in 1848. Although those in the know

When gold was discovered here at Sutter's Mill in California, people from the rest of the country and from all over the world journeyed to the West. Most were men, many of whom left their wives and children temporarily in the hopes of providing for their family.

tried to keep the information hidden, word soon leaked out. The next year, thousands of men—and a few women—from all over the world rushed in to the California gold country to strike it rich. The sudden population explosion and resultant social changes created new opportunities for some women, new tragedies for others.

With Americans rushing to grab a piece of the newly expanded territorial pie, old sectional disputes between North and South again came to the fore. With the Missouri Compromise of 1820, Congress had precariously balanced the number of slave and free states. Northerners, whether abolitionist or merely opposed to the presence of blacks, were agreed that they did not want to see the spread of slavery into the West. Southerners saw expansion of slavery as the only way to maintain their political and economic influence. These controversies would help speed the two sides toward civil war in 1861.

Amidst all these events of national and international significance, few Americans took notice of a small group of women meeting in Seneca Falls, New York. But there, in the heart of the Burned-over

Lucretia and James Mott are seated at far right in the front row of this portrait of the executive committee of the Philadelphia Anti-Slavery Society in 1851. Mott had used her experience as an abolitionist leader to help organize the women's rights convention at Seneca Falls in 1848.

District, Lucretia Mott and Elizabeth Cady Stanton organized the first convention for women's rights in the United States. Fortunately, while others were looking elsewhere, the women delegates retained a sense of the history that they were making and carefully recorded the proceedings. Thus we are able today to add the Seneca Falls Convention to the list of revolutionary occurrences in 1848.

Although Mott and Stanton had been earnest in their desire to organize a women's rights meeting, they both found themselves burdened with numerous other duties. Mott continued to be a leader in the abolitionist movement and to raise her children and care for her husband. Stanton, recently married to journalist and reformer Henry Stanton, soon found herself overwhelmed with duties as a new wife and mother.

Young Elizabeth had been a child of privilege; as a teenager she had attended Emma Willard's seminary in Troy. The Stantons had originally settled in Boston, a center for abolitionist and literary activities. Here Elizabeth Stanton was in her element, establishing friendships with Lydia Maria Child, Abby Kelley Foster, Maria Weston Chapman, Frederick Douglass, and other leading abolitionists. Henry Stanton found the wet Boston climate debilitating, however, and he moved his family to the small town of Seneca Falls.

In Boston, Elizabeth Stanton had been able to take advantage of city conveniences to make her life easier. Once in Seneca Falls, she had to work at numerous difficult tasks that her money had once paid for. Even when she could hire domestic help, she found herself a prisoner of the household. She later recalled, "I now fully understood the practical difficulties most women had to contend with in the isolated household, and the impossibility of woman's best development if in contact the chief part of her life with servants and children."

Fortunately, she made good use of this lesson. She later recalled:

Emerson says: "A healthy discontent is a the first step to progress." The general discontent I felt with women's portion as wife, mother, housekeeper, physician, and spiritual guide, the chaotic condition into which everything fell with her constant supervision, and the wearied, anxious look of the majority of women, impressed me with the strong feeling that some active measures should be taken to remedy the wrongs of society in general and of women in particular.

Elizabeth Cady Stanton holds her daughter, Harriot. Although Stanton did not denounce her role as wife and mother, she felt that women should be allowed to participate more fully in society and should not be confined to the home.

Luckily, Lucretia Mott was visiting the area soon after Stanton came to this understanding of her life and her life's purpose. Reunited with Mott, Stanton was further comforted by Mott's sister, Martha Wright, and Mott's friends Jane Hunt and Mary Ann McClintock—Quakers all. In the company of these women, Stanton "poured out," as she wrote in her autobiography, "the torrent of my long accumulating discontent, with such vehemence and indignation that I stirred myself, as well as the rest of the party, to do and dare something."

The result of this fateful meeting was an advertisement, placed in the *Seneca County Courier,* announcing a "Woman's Rights Convention—A convention to discuss the social, civil and religious rights of women will be held in the Wesleyan Chapel, Seneca Falls, New York, the 19th and 20th of July current." The advertisement noted, "During the first day the meeting will be held exclusively for women, who are earnestly invited to attend." The advertisement also offered a figure of national prominence, noting that "Lucretia Mott of Philadelphia and other ladies and gentlemen will address the convention."

Because nobody had organized a women's rights convention before, the five women had to make things up as they went along. Nonetheless, they were able to draw on the organizing tactics, administrative skills, and ideology of equal rights that they had developed in the abolitionist movement. For the Declaration of Sentiments of the convention, Stanton drew heavily on the Declaration of Independence. If it worked for the forefathers of America, Stanton figured, it would serve the foremothers of women's rights quite nicely.

Perhaps it was the Declaration of Independence's call for the rights and responsibilities of citizenship that inspired Stanton to make the radical demand for a woman's right to vote. Henry Stanton, considered a radical abolitionist and free-thinker, was appalled. He threatened to leave town if his wife persisted in making this demand, and he kept to his word. The idea of woman suffrage at first proved too much for even the forward-thinking Lucretia Mott, who responded to Stanton's proposal by writing, "Thou will make us ridiculous. We must go slowly." Stanton was encouraged to persist, however, by the support of the eminent abolitionist and ex-slave Frederick Douglass. Knowing Douglass's support would carry a lot of moral weight, Stanton decided to include the call for woman suffrage, or

Henry Brewster Stanton, a prominent abolitionist, generally supported his wife's activities but initially balked at Elizabeth Cady Stanton's support of woman suffrage.

the right to vote, in the resolutions.

Stanton and Mott were concerned that they might end up addressing their own circle of friends. But the vast changes that had begun early in the 19th century had taken root in the fertile ground of the Burned-over District. From 50 miles around, people came by cart, by horse, and on foot—more than 300 in all—to take part in this first official step toward liberation. The convention even attracted dozens of men, who after some discussion, were allowed to participate on the first day.

Perhaps we can take Charlotte Woodward's story as typical of those who chose to brave public ridicule and join in this groundbreaking event. Woodward, just 19 at the time, lived on a nearby farm but dreamed of one day working as a typesetter. It was an impossible dream, she knew—but then, who would have dreamed of a women's rights convention being held in Seneca Falls? When Woodward first read the fateful notice in the *Seneca Courier,* however, she began to believe in the power of dreams. While some of her neighbors did indeed laugh at the notion of women assembling to discuss their supposed rights, Woodward found six other brave souls to attend

The Stanton house in Seneca Falls, New York. After living in Boston, Elizabeth Cady Stanton found this rural community stifling and came to the realization that the role of wife and mother was not sufficient for many women.

This sheet music, published in 1916, envisions a day when women will be allowed to vote. American women first demanded the right to vote in 1848, but their dream was not realized until 1920.

the meeting with her. As they set out in their wagon, they wondered if any other women would dare to attend. But their spirits soared as they spied other vehicles making their way toward the convention hall. Suddenly, they realized they were no longer alone.

Liberation does not come quickly, however, nor easily. Among those stalwart women, none was willing to take up the gavel and lead the meeting; that honor was given to James Mott, Lucretia's husband. And when it came time to vote on the resolutions, all passed unanimously except No. 9—the resolution calling for women's enfranchisement, or the right to vote. After much debate, however, that passed as well, and the modern woman suffrage movement was born.

Some 72 years later, Congress passed and the states ratified the 19th Amendment to the U.S. Constitution, ensuring that "the right of the citizens of the United States shall not be denied or abridged . . . on account of sex." Only one woman who signed the Declaration of Principles—19-year-old Charlotte Woodward—was still alive to vote in the Presidential election of 1920.

If Seneca Falls was a revolutionary event, it was also one that would take a good bit of time to make its impact known. Indeed, the reverberations set off by those five women sitting around their kitchen table—the same table that now stands honored in the Smithsonian Institution—are still being felt today. For a revolution is not won or lost in a few days time, or a few years. Its legacy lasts for generations, a continued source of inspiration for some, antagonism for others, and reflection for all.

CHRONOLOGY

1809	First Native American Catholic convent established by Mother Seton in Maryland
1814	Boston Manufacturing Company, first cotton mill to use the power loom, begins production at Waltham, Massachusetts
1818	Colored Female Religious and Moral Society of Salem founded
1821	Emma Willard opens Troy Female Seminary
1824	Charles Finney initiates revivals in the "Burned-over District"
1827	Cherokee constitution bars women from voting in tribal matters
1832	Female Antislavery Society of Salem founded
1833	Oberlin College founded; Philadelphia Female Antislavery Society founded by Lucretia Mott, Charlotte Forten, and others
1834	Ursuline convent in Charlestown, Massachusetts, is burned to the ground; New York Female Moral Reform Society founded; First all-woman strike by mill workers, in Lowell, Massachusetts
1836	Angelina Grimké publishes *An Appeal to the Christian Women of the South*
1837	Sarah Josepha Hale assumes editorship of *Godey's Lady's Book;* Mary Lyon opens Mount Holyoke Female Seminary
1838	Mob burns down abolitionist Philadelphia Hall; Sarah Grimké publishes *Letters on the Equality of the Sexes and the Condition of Women*
1840	American Antislavery Society accepts women as members; World Antislavery Convention refuses to seat Lucretia Mott as an American delegate
1841	Catharine Beecher writes *A Treatise on Domestic Economy;* American Antislavery Society splits over admission of women members and other controversies
1843	Joseph Smith claims revelation from God instructing Mormons to adopt polygamy
1845	Margaret Fuller publishes *Women in the Nineteenth Century*
1847	Narcissa Whitman, her husband, and fellow missionaries slain by Cayuse war party
1848	Seneca Falls women's rights convention

FURTHER READING

A Note on Sources

In the interest of readability, the volumes in this series include no discussion of historiography and no footnotes. As works of synthesis and overview, however, they are greatly indebted to the research and writing of other historians. The principal works drawn on in this volume are among the books listed below.

General Histories

Blasingame, John W. *The Slave Community: Plantation Life in the Antebellum South.* Rev. ed. New York: Oxford University Press, 1979.

Boyer, Paul. *Urban Masses and Moral Order in America, 1820–1920.* Cambridge: Harvard University Press, 1978.

Faragher, John Mack. *Sugar Creek: Life on the Illinois Prairie.* New Haven: Yale University Press, 1986.

Genovese, Eugene. *Roll, Jordan, Roll: The World the Slaves Made.* New York: Vintage Books, 1976.

Gutman, Herbert. *The Black Family in Slavery and Freedom.* New York: Pantheon Books, 1976.

Monroy, Douglas. *Thrown among Strangers: The Making of Mexican Culture in Frontier California.* Berkeley: University of California Press, 1990.

Ryan, Mary P. *The Cradle of the Middle Class: The Family in Oneida County, 1780–1835.* New York: Cambridge University Press, 1983.

Walters, Ronald G. *American Reformers, 1815–1860.* New York: Hill & Wang, 1978.

Histories of Women

Clinton, Catherine. *Plantation Mistress: Women's World in the Old South.* New York: Vintage Books, 1982.

Cott, Nancy F. *The Bonds of Womanhood: "Woman's Sphere" in New England, 1780–1835.* New Haven: Yale University Press, 1977.

Cott, Nancy F., and Elizabeth H. Pleck. *A Heritage of Her Own: Toward a New Social History of American Women.* New York: Simon & Schuster, 1979.

Cowen, Ruth Schwartz. *More Work for Mother: The Ironies of Household Technology from the Open Hearth to the Microwave.* New York: Basic Books, 1983.

Dublin, Thomas. *Women at Work: The Transformation of Work and Community in Lowell, Massachusetts, 1826–1860.* New York: Columbia University Press, 1979.

DuBois, Ellen Carol, and Vicki L. Ruiz. *Unequal Sisters: A Multi-Cultural Reader in U.S. Women's History.* New York: Routledge, 1990.

Evans, Sara M. *Born for Liberty: A History of Women in America.* New York: Free Press, 1989.

Flexner, Eleanor. *Century of Struggle: The Woman's Rights Movement in the United States.* Cambridge: Harvard University Press, 1975.

Fox-Genovese, Elizabeth. *Within the Plantation Household: Black and White Women in the Old South*. Chapel Hill: University of North Carolina Press, 1988.

Jensen, Joan. *Loosening the Bonds: Mid-Atlantic Farm Women, 1750–1850*. New Haven: Yale University Press, 1986.

Kessler-Harris, Alice. *Out to Work: A History of Wage-Earning Women in the United States*. New York: Oxford University Press, 1982.

Lebsock, Suzanne. *Free Women of Petersburg: Status and Culture in a Southern Town, 1784–1865*. New York: Norton, 1985.

Melder, Keith E. *Beginnings of Sisterhood: The American Woman's Rights Movement, 1800–1860*. New York: Schocken Books, 1977.

Rothman, Ellen K. *Hands and Hearts: A History of Courtship in America*. New York: Basic Books, 1984.

Ryan, Mary P. *Womanhood in America: From Colonial Times to the Present*. 3rd ed. New York: Franklin Watts, 1983.

Scott, Anne Firor. *Natural Allies: Women's Associations in American History*. Urbana: University of Illinois Press, 1991.

Stansell, Christine. *City of Women: Sex and Class in New York, 1789–1860*. Urbana: University of Illinois Press, 1987.

White, Deborah Gray. *Ar'n't I a Woman: Female Slaves in the Plantation South*. New York: Norton, 1985.

Biographies, Autobiographies, and First-Person Accounts

Bazandall, Rosalyn, et al., eds. *America's Working Women: A Documentary History—1600 to the Present*. New York: Vintage Books, 1976.

Buhle, Mari Jo, and Paul Buhle, eds. *The Concise History of Woman Suffrage: Selections from the Classic Work of Stanton, Anthony, Gage, and Harper*. Urbana: University of Illinois Press, 1978.

Cott, Nancy F., ed. *Root of Bitterness: Documents of the Social History of American Women*. New York: Dutton, 1972.

Dublin, Thomas. *Farm to Factory: Women's Letters, 1830–1860*. New York: Columbia University Press, 1981.

Eckhardt, Celia. *Fanny Wright: Rebel in America*. Cambridge: Harvard University Press, 1984.

Greene, Dana, ed. *Lucretia Mott: Her Complete Speeches and Sermons*. New York: E. Mellon Press, 1980.

Hays, Eleanor Rice. *Morning Star: A Biography of Lucy Stone, 1818–1893*. New York: Octagon, 1978.

Lerner, Gerda. *The Grimke Sisters from South Carolina: Pioneers for Women's Rights and Abolition*. New York: Houghton Mifflin, 1967.

Lerner, Gerda, ed. *Black Women in White America: A Documentary History*. New York: Pantheon Books, 1979.

Sklar, Kathryn Kish. *Catharine Beecher: A Study in American Domesticity*. New Haven: Yale University Press, 1973.

Stanton, Elizabeth Cady. *Eighty Years and More: Reminiscences, 1815–1897*. New York: Schocken Books, 1971.

Sterling, Dorothy. *We Are Your Sisters: Black Women in the Nineteenth Century*. New York: Norton, 1984.

INDEX

Picture Credits

Collection of the Albany Institute of History & Art: 21; Archdiocese of Boston Archives: 68; Bishop Hill Historic Site, Illinois Historic Preservation Agency: cover; Boston Athenaeum: 27, 54, 55, 56, 112, 124-T, 124-B, 125; California State Library, California Section: 76, 131; The Chrysler Museum, Norfolk, Virginia. Gift of Edgar William and Bernice Chrysler Garbisch, 80.181.20: 7; Denver Public Library, Western History Department: 88; Hancock Shaker Village, Pittsfield, Mass./Paul Rocheleau, photographer: 75; Historical Society of York County, York, Pennsylvania: 43-L; Courtesy of the Illinois State Historical Library: 71; Joslyn Art Museum, Omaha, Nebraska: 92, 93; Library of Congress: 10, 19, 22, 23, 26, 34, 39, 42, 44, 45-T, 62, 64, 69, 96, 100, 101, 102, 113, 114, 119, 120, 121, 127, 133, 134; Library Company of Philadelphia: 61; Lowell Historical Society, Lowell, Mass.: 109; Massachusetts State Archives, Boston: 106; Mount Holyoke College Art Museum, South Hadley, Mass.: 51-T; Mount Holyoke College Library/Archives: 51-B; Museum of American Textile History: frontispiece, 30, 38, 40, 45-B, 104, 107; Museum of the Cherokee Indian: 80; Museum of the City of New York, *New York by Gaslight, "Hooking a Victim,"* circa 1850. Acc. No. 37.361.423. Gift of Karl Schmidt: 97; Museum of the Confederacy, Richmond, Virginia. Eleanor S. Brockenbrough Library: 29; Photo Courtesy of the Museum of the Confederacy, Richmond, Virginia. Private Collection: 25; New Bedford Whaling Museum: 17; Collection of The New-York Historical Society: 79, 122; Oberlin College Archives: 52, 53, 58-L, 58-R; Oklahoma Historical Society, Archives and Manuscripts Division: 81; Oneida County Historical Society, Utica, New York: 59, 60; Oregon Historical Society: 84 (ORH.1645), 85 (ORH.12760), 87 (ORH.1644); Courtesy of the Pennsylvania Academy of the Fine Arts, Philadelphia. Gift of Paul Beck, Jr.: 18; The Saint Louis Art Museum, Purchase and Funds Given by Decorative Arts Society: 46; Schomburg Center for Research in Black Culture, New York Public Library, Astor, Lenox and Tilden Foundations: 13, 41, 117; Seaver Center for Western History Research, Natural History Museum of Los Angeles County: 91; From the archives of the Seneca Falls Historical Society: 135; Shaker Museum, Old Chatham, New York: 73, 74; Smithsonian Institution: 8, 20, 32, 78, 110, 118, 123, 128, 136; Society of California Pioneers: 89; Sophia Smith Collection, Smith College, Northampton, Mass.: 48, 132; South Caroliniana Library. University of South Carolina: 65; Utah State Historical Society, Photograph Collection: 70, 72: Virginia State Library and Archives: 15, Courtesy the Winterthur Library, Printed Book and Periodical Collection: 36; Courtesy Winterthur Museum: 67.

Michael Goldberg is assistant professor of liberal studies at the University of Washington at Bothell. He is the author of *An Army of Women: Gender, Politics and Power in Gilded-Age Kansas,* which is part of the *Reconfiguring American History* series published by John Hopkins University Press, and a contributor to the *Dictionary of American Biography.* Dr. Goldberg previously taught at New Mexico Tech and Yale University. He holds a Ph.D. in American studies from Yale and a B.A. in American studies from the University of California, Santa Cruz.

Nancy F. Cott is Stanley Woodward Professor of history and American studies at Yale University. She is the author of *The Bonds of Womanhood: "Woman's Sphere" in New England 1780–1835, The Grounding of Modern Feminism,* and *A Woman Making History: Mary Ritter Beard Through Her Letters*; editor of *Root of Bitterness: Documents of the Social History of American Women*; and coeditor of *A Heritage of Her Own: Toward a New Social History of American Women.*